COUNTRY STYLE

CHOOSING
COLOUR & PATTERN

COUNTRY STYLE

CHOOSING
COLOUR & PATTERN

WARD LOCK

A WARD LOCK BOOK

First published in the UK 1995 by Ward Lock,
Wellington House, 125 Strand, London WC2R 0BB.

A Cassell Imprint

Copyright © Eaglemoss Publications Limited 1995
Based on The Country Look

Front cover pictures: EWA (top let), J.C.Scotto (top right), Steve
Tanner/Eaglemoss (bottom left), EWA (bottom right). Back cover
picture: Sanderson.

A British Library Cataloguing in Publication Data block for
this book may be obtained from the British Library

ISBN 0 7063 7437 1
Printed and bound in Hong Kong

CONTENTS

Understanding colour

Some people are blessed with a natural feeling for colour. They instinctively know which colours will go together, how to balance tones and when to introduce a contrasting accent shade. They can effortlessly mix and match colours to create a comfy bedroom or a stylish living room. For the rest of us, it is more often than not a case of trial and error. But it needn't be, if you take a little time to understand a few simple rules. With the help of a colour wheel, you can analyse colour relationships and learn why a particular arrangement of colours work. This will help you to use colour with confidence and to plan or rectify a colour scheme when your intuition lets you down.

▼ *Contrasts and harmonies*
A rich palette of colours is assembled in this arrangement of full-blown roses. The yellow, orange, apricot and pink coloured blooms relate harmoniously because they come from the same sector of the colour wheel. The sharp green, which comes from the opposite side of the wheel, provides a contrast.

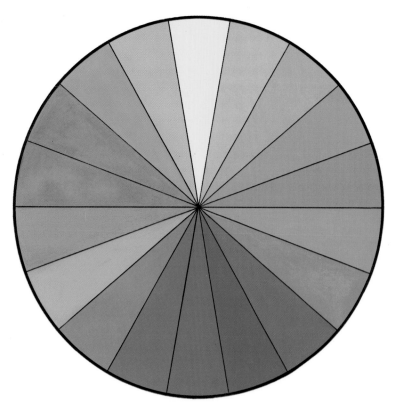

The colour wheel

The colour wheel is a traditional diagrammatic illustration of colour relationships, and a useful aid to decorating your home. The three primary colours are red, yellow and blue. Colours which fall between two primaries have a harmonious relationship, while those that occur opposite one another on the wheel are complementary. Colours on either side of a primary become less harmonious the further apart they are.

▶ A rosy glow
Here, a rich and exuberant scheme combines cerise, cherry and brick reds. This is not an obvious combination of colours, but they work well together because of their harmonious relationship. You will find them all located between red and orange on the colour wheel. If you look closely at the picture you will find that the colours have a similar tonal value, so that none overwhelms the others. In fact, the only tonal contrast is provided by the dark wooden bedstead.

▲ Sea and sky
The slightly muted shades of blue and blue-green are a particularly soothing range of colours. They are very compatible and can be used boldly and freely in creating a traditional country setting. In this cottage kitchen, the sky blue predominates on the walls and ceiling, acting as the perfect foil for the blue-green paintwork on the door and window.

Small touches of a strong reddish purple act as a sparky accent colour in the overall scheme, on the wall by the door as a dado band, on the tartan curtain under the sink and in the heather on the table.

Harmonious colours

Most people find colour schemes based on a limited range of colours pleasing and comfortable to live with. Fortunately, these harmonious colour schemes are also the easiest to put into practice without taking too many design risks.

Monochrome schemes

The simplest kind of harmony relies on arrangements based on a single colour. These are virtually foolproof colour schemes which share many of the qualities of a neutral scheme, in that they are restful, because the colours blend well, and work in almost any location or style of house.

If you want to develop a one-colour scheme, start from the colour of the existing upholstery or an ornament, or even a new textile that appeals to you. Even within a single colour, you can find a rich variety of subtly different colours called shades, which range from cool to warm, through muted to intense. The paler and darker versions of the same shade are known as tones.

You could, for example, choose a pale shade for the walls and ceiling which will reflect the light. You can then add interest and emphasis by using darker or lighter tones of the same colour to pick out architectural details like skirting boards and door frames. Still richer or more intense shades of the same colour can be used to draw attention to a particularly attractive feature such as an intricate moulding.

Related harmonies

The second kind of harmonious scheme is made up from groups of colours that lie between the primary colours on the colour wheel. Look, for example, at the colours between blue and yellow and you will find a range of blue-greens and green-blues. The eye runs easily between them without an abrupt transition. Even when they are taken out of sequence, a group of these related colours always goes well together.

The scope of this scheme can be considerably extended by introducing shades of these colours in lighter and darker tones and more muted mixtures. Once again, you need to work in gentle steps between tones, to eliminate visual jolts. Save extreme contrasts for small touches of emphasis. A very light or very dark tone of one of the colours you are using can become an accent to give a lift to an otherwise restrained scheme.

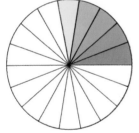

▶ Nasturtium bright
In this sunny, summery corner, terracotta and sunflower yellow checks sit happily together on a cushion and throw. By working with a restricted palette of colours, it has been possible to create a very well co-ordinated arrangement which still has plenty of vitality.

If you study the picture, you will find that the main colours are present in different tones on various items; pale terracotta and daffodil yellow feature in the cushion, while deeper tones of the same shades are woven in the throw. As the odd colour, turquoise sizzles against a red from the other side of the colour wheel.

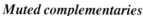

Complementary colours

Many people want more excitement from their surroundings than the essentially soothing and restrained settings created by monochrome schemes or those based on adjacent, harmonious colours. You may favour calmness in some rooms, like the bedrooms or hallway, but seek a more energetic look in the living room, play room or kitchen.

The complementary pairs – the colours opposite each other on the colour wheel – provide an effective way of creating a satisfying colour scheme which has a bit more zest. Their special relationship means that when they are used together they bring out the best in each other. So red used with green has more punch than it has on its own.

Schemes for the adventurous

Complementary pairings from opposite sides of the colour wheel are inspiring if you want to introduce visual drama into your surroundings. For a vivid scheme, look to the brightest shades, like the colours shown on our colour wheel. These high contrast schemes can be tricky and need to be handled with care. Use the colours in different tones, and introduce neutrals such as grey, white, beige or brown to take some of the harsh edge off the arrangement.

Muted complementaries

Some of the most enjoyable colour schemes can be devised around the less strident complementary pairs. These muted shades are nearer to those seen in nature, earth colours like brown and terracotta and dried flower colours like lilac, pale blue, peach and primrose.

Terracotta finds its complementary partner in a bright blue. Yellow ochre looks good with a pale blue. Khaki green is set off by the purple of iris. The possibilities of such pairings are almost infinite. Using them, you can create colourful schemes which are easy to live with, but never boring.

Complementaries as accents

Accent colours are introduced in small quantities to add spice to a scheme. The complementary of the main colour is a particularly effective accent. A splash of red in a largely green scheme will result in both colours being experienced more intensely. The red will look redder, the green greener.

The warm colours, which are more advancing than the cool shades, have considerable impact even in small quantities. So very small amounts of red will liven up a green room, while larger amounts of green will be required to have the same impact in a red room.

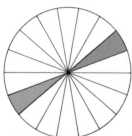

▼ Terracotta and sky blue *Terracotta and orange find their complementary partners in the blue range. These colours have a wonderful resonance and bring out the best in each other - the terracotta looks richer and the sky blue brighter. They can be used as accent colours to each other, or as the basis of a colour scheme, in a kitchen, for example, where blue paint is paired with quarry tiles.*

◀ **Magenta and green** *Magenta and the cool reds are precisely complemented by various shades of bright green. Here, the sparkling colours of the books and stationery on the desk, and the more sombre, muted tones in the floral wallpaper and fireplace, exploit these relationships very successfully. It illustrates beautifully how toning complementary partnerships hold good regardless of the strength of the colours.*

▼ **Yellow and purple**
This is a particularly lively pairing of complementary colours that can be used to produce some very rich and exciting effects in decorating. In these wacky fabrics, it is interesting to see how well a whole range of vibrant colours work together to produce a joyful outcome. The grey cats introduce a vital neutral note.

11

Problem-solving with colour

A knowledge of colour relationships will help you to solve interior design problems. Take a common dilemma. A room is newly redecorated but it still doesn't feel quite right. You have chosen harmonious colours from the same sector of the colour wheel, so they should go together. It may be that there are too many contrasts of tone and shade, so the eye is constantly jolted as it moves from one area to another.

To remedy this, you can ensure a gentler gradation from one colour to the next, and restore a harmonious balance to the room, by introducing a few intermediate shades and tones into the scheme on cushions, shades and rugs.

▼▶ Seeing red – or green and red
Sometimes, a colour scheme is disappointing because it plays too safe and ends up looking rather dull. In which case, a harmonious tonal contrast can be deliberately introduced as light relief. That is exactly what has happened in this vividly pink room. Although it could never be tame, the shock of other reds brings it to life.

Another solution is to inject the appropriate complementary colour from the opposite side of the colour wheel – in this case green – to add the necessary verve to the scheme. Here, the green in the floral fabric works with the red in the tablecloth to give the setting a lift.

Choosing a colour scheme

Colour is the most important element in any decorative scheme, yet it is an area that most of us shy away from. It is the most exciting, the most flexible and the least expensive aspect of home design and yet we so often opt for neutral colours with the occasional splash of colour or pattern. Colour sets the mood and style of a room, and gives it personality. It affects the impact the room has on people, the way they feel in it and the way they behave. And the colours you use will reflect your personality.

▼ **Helping plan a colour scheme**
There are many aids to help you select the right colours. Paint manufacturers produce colour charts, and shops will let you have samples of papers and fabrics. Magazines and catalogues are another invaluable source of inspiration.

Practical colour choices

Colour also has practical functions: the choice of colour can make a room seem larger or smaller, cooler or warmer. Colour also has strong associations in our minds. For example, pink is seen as a clean colour and is often used in bathrooms, while red, brown and green, which are associated with food, are favourite colours in kitchens.

Many of our reactions to colour are derived from associations with the natural world – greens and blues are seen as cool and soothing, while reds and yellows are seen as warm and energetic.

Starting from scratch

Most of us have dreamt of having the opportunity to design and decorate a room from scratch, having an absolutely free hand. But, surprisingly, this is the most difficult task of all – it can be like the painter who is faced with a blank canvas. Fortunately, in real life, decisions are usually made within an existing scheme.

If you are considering a new decorative scheme the first thing to do is to look long and hard at the room you are going to decorate, listing its good and bad points, and thinking about things like lighting and how the room will be used. To help you do this, answer the questions in the checklist overleaf and start from there.

Ways to choose colour

There are a number of tactics you can adopt to choose your colour scheme.

Personal preference We all have favourite colours. If yours is yellow, for example, and the room is very light, the colour may be too much for the room. Think about using yellow in a patterned fabric for the curtains or soft furnishings instead of the walls.

Catalogues The major soft furnishing companies and paint and wallpaper manufacturers co-ordinate their colours and patterns, often with a style in mind. Looking at their catalogues, you may see a colour scheme that you like. Try to reproduce it using their products or something close to them.

Start with the accessories There are many accessories that fit into the country style such as dried flowers and china and often their colours will help you pick your favourite from a shade card. Use them as a starting point. A treasured ornament or vase could be another starting point, or perhaps a patterned sofa or rug. In the bedroom, use bed linen as a basis for the scheme.

Three points to remember

Light affects the way you perceive colours. For example, a green which looks muted and has a blue tinge under strip lighting in the showroom, may look warmer and more yellow in a sunny, south-facing room. A deep, holly-leaf green will look even darker and richer in a dark room, but will lose much of its intensity in a brightly-lit room. This is why it is so important to try out a large sample of the colour in the room in which you intend to use it.

Colours are affected and modified by surrounding colours, so while a bright blue may kill a subtle pink, a paler blue will look wonderful. This is because mixtures of colours of equal tone look good together – pastel pinks, yellows and peaches, for example.

If, when you have bought the paint, the particular colour looks too bright, you can create a balance by adding small amounts of white or black paint, mixing well and testing. This takes courage but the results can be rewarding.

Combinations of strong, bright reds, yellows and blues also look harmonious and well balanced. This is because they have the same depth of colour and brightness.

The amount of colour affects the way you see it. While it might be difficult to live with four walls of bright orange or strong pink, splashes of these colours add zest to an all-white or single-colour scheme.

COLOUR SCHEME CHECKLIST

There are some general dos and don'ts that you should consider before you decide on your new colour scheme.

Is it a frequently used area?	YES	Choose peaceful, easy colours on walls; patterned or neutral flooring.
	NO	A bold splash of colour is a nice change; elegant pastels or cream can be used where they won't get too dirty.
Does it face north?	YES	Warm it up with red, sunny yellow or peach.
	NO	Cool blues and greens will be balanced by the warm light.
Is the ceiling low?	YES	Paint it white or cream to give the room height; a vertically striped paper would help.
	NO	You could take the wall colour/paper right over the ceiling for a total look.
Is the room smaller than you would like?	YES	Keep to clear, pale tones, small or self patterns – go for texture to add interest.
	NO	Link different parts of the room by splashes of the same strong tone against bold contrasts.
Does it have enough light?	YES	You can choose dark colours and rich woods like mahogany.
	NO	Reflect the light with white/cream walls, pine or light wood and a mirror.
Is it a 'first impressions' area such as an entrance hall or lobby?	YES	Give a welcome glow with warm pinks, reds and happy yellow.
	NO	Indulge yourself – choose your favourite colour.
Is it crowded, with furniture, knick-knacks and people?	YES	Keep it simple. A one-colour scheme to act as a background to the chaos.
	NO	Add interest and life with bright splashes of colour and strong patterns.
Do you or any of your family work in it?	YES	Be business-like. Plain uncluttered surroundings are less distracting.
	NO	Pretty soft pastels give a restful look; dress it up with florals.
Do children spend a lot of time in the room?	YES	Stimulate their senses with bright, interesting patterns and bold colours.
	NO	Check on any pet hates of the rest of the family before you do anything final.

A single-colour scheme

One of the simplest ways of working out a single-colour scheme is to start with one major item and use a limited palette of colours. Start collecting samples of paints, fabrics and carpets. Look for your chosen colour and related tones of other colours. Look for small, subtle patterns as these are easier to mix and match than stronger, brighter ones.

If you are too rigorous about finding related tones and colours, the result could be boring. Add interest with subtle textures, apply the paint with a broken colour paint effect on the walls, for example, or a berber weave carpet.

Splashes of a contrasting colour lift a scheme. In a blue room, for example, orange cushions or a woven rug with orange shades will add a touch of warmth and excitement to the scheme. (Orange is on the warm side of the spectrum – a little will have a lot of impact.) All these separate elements come together to create a satisfying whole – even flowers can be part of the scheme.

▼ **Fresh green scheme**
A The freshness and greenness is picked up in the key component – the delightful green gingham covers on the simple, stylish high-backed dining chairs. The roman blinds are made in crisp white linen.
B Emulsion paint on the walls and ceiling is a good choice. The walls are pale apple green and the ceiling is white with a hint of green which picks up the predominant colour and creates an illusion of height.
C The other elements maintain the single-colour theme – framed prints are of verdant spring and summer foliage, the glass table has metal legs with a bluey-green patina and a brass urn has a turquoise surface.
D The warm, honeyed tones of the parquet floor act as a counterweight to the prevailing cool tones. Buff paint is used to pick out the panelling on the corner cupboard.

Starting from a pattern

By using a multi-coloured pattern as your jumping-off point you can create a more ambitious colour scheme using the expertise and colour sense of the designer.

The people who design fabrics and wallpapers are experts at handling colour, they know what goes with what, and which proportions work best, so by pulling out colours from a pattern and using them in the same proportions you can create a harmonious scheme.

Manufacturers supply ranges of co-ordinating fabrics – large prints with small prints and plains and stripes – which provide ready-made solutions to mix-and-match requirements.

Floral patterns

The key to this room with its warm, rosy and russet colours, is the comfortable armchair, covered in a large floral pattern. The main colours on the pattern have been used as a starting point to build the colour scheme. Here the large golden-headed flowers are the dominant element. This is matched by the golden tones of the polished pine floorboards – the single largest area of solid colour in the room.

On the walls a smaller sprigged pattern in the same colourways echoes the larger print with a still smaller floral wallpaper border hung at picture rail level. The rich coral on the walls of the hallway and above the picture rail adds warmth and drama to an otherwise simple scheme.

Coral is used for the curtains which are self-patterned, adding subtle texture. This coral note has been drawn from a minor theme in the main fabric, but contributes a main theme to the room decor. Remember that colours used near a window have a more powerful influence as the colour tints the light which permeates the whole room. Here the coral curtains give the room a warm glow.

Using the colours matched by the fabric designer gives you the confidence to put together unusual colours.

▼ **Co-ordinated fabric and papers**
Although the patterns are different the colours all blend in this range.

▲ Pattern used as the starting point

A strongly patterned fabric is the key to this colour scheme.

A The warm ochre and coral of the floral print on the armchair are the basis for the rest of the colours used in this scheme.

B The pinky-red of the carnations is picked up in the rich coral walls and damask curtains. The upholstery fabric has been used for the tie-back.

C The floors are warm polished natural wood.

D A co-ordinating fabric, wallpaper and border in a smaller floral bouquet print keep within the colour scheme.

E Floral prints in antiqued golden frames pick up the theme colours.

17

What colours do you like?

For a lucky few, choosing colours is easy. They are born with a natural sense of colour, and can remember shades of a colour so precisely, they can match a pinky-red without a sample, while the rest of us would arrive home with a pillar-box red that was quite wrong. However, some of us don't even know what colours we like, because we have never really thought about it.

Faced with re-decorating a room, don't be overcome with panic and take the easy way out by going for what you had before. Spend time thinking about it and looking for ideas – you may discover that you have strong colour preferences.

Start by looking in your wardrobe – your clothes probably fall into a few distinctive colour groups. Another trick is to leaf through magazines and catalogues marking the pages which show room schemes that you like. A few days later, look through the pages you have marked – you will find that these too fall into definite colour categories.

Looking for inspiration

There are many ways of finding a hook for a colour scheme. Look at the objects you gather around you. For example, have you got a collection of pots and jugs, or do you have paintings or prints on your walls. All these things can be used as the basis of a colour scheme – they also reveal your colour preferences.

If you still aren't sure, experiment by introducing small touches of colour – this is particularly effective in plain rooms. Look around for objects in the colours you are contemplating using – pots, paintings or even flowers. Arrange them in the room and live with them for a while to see how you feel about living with it permanently.

▲ **Blue and white details**
You don't need to spend a great deal of money to bring colour into your home. A plain white bathroom is transformed by adding pale blue baskets, pots and a soap holder. The blue hydrangeas are an inspired touch.

◀ **Pastels and primaries**
The spring colours of this room reflect the owner's taste which is revealed in the painting on the wall, and in the collection of glass vases and plates on the shelf beneath.

Sunrise and sunset colours

Some rooms seem warm and inviting, even on a chilly day when the inside temperature is not particularly high; but other rooms are never cosy and cheerful no matter how high the heating. The solution to this apparent contradiction lies in the colour scheme. Human beings are particularly sensitive to the effect of colour and no sooner does the eye take in a particular colour than the subconscious gets to work, raking up a complicated network of associations – some going back to early childhood – which can affect us both emotionally and physically.

If you want a room to to look warm and cheerful, it is sensible to choose colours that make you feel warm and cheerful. These are the hot colours – reds, yellows and oranges. From them come the warm colours – the colours we associate with sunrise and sunset – ranging from the palest pinks and primroses, to deep shades of peach, rich russets and pinky, brick reds. The down-to-earth Victorians knew perfectly well what they were about when they papered their dining rooms in deep reds and oranges; they felt these colours created a sense of well-being and warmth, which in turn helped them to feel comfortable, and allowed them to enjoy their food.

There is also a gradation between warm and cool colours – the blues and greens: some warm colours are cooler than others, while some cool colours are at the warm end of the cool spectrum. You can only really appreciate the subtle differences by comparing colours side by side. But these differences are nevertheless important, when you come to choosing whether to paint your walls pink or yellow as these large areas of colour will create quite a big impact.

▼ Wonderful warmth
Reds, oranges, pinks and golden yellows are the colours of fire and sunshine, of autumn and summer. Use them in patterns and plains to warm a bleak room or make a large room seem cosy.

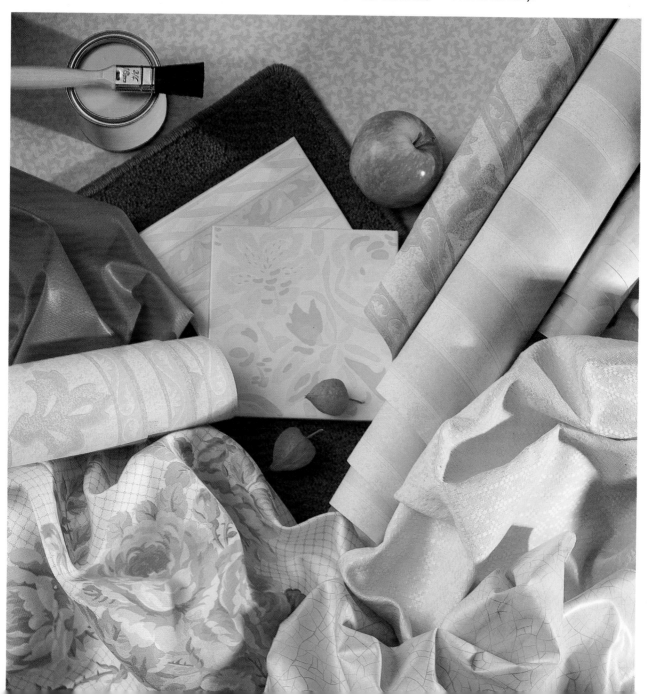

▲ Peachy pink for a bathroom
Subtle shades from the warm side of the spectrum combine to create a pretty and cosy bathroom. Peachy pink above the dado rail and on the ceiling is teamed with a sandy shade below, and pale cream gloss on the woodwork. These sand and cream shades are picked up in the marble-effect floor tiles. Deep pink towels, and drapes at the window add a splash of colour.

▼ Rich rust in a traditional kitchen
Rust-red gloss paint has been applied over anaglypta wallpaper to create a kitchen which is warm, comfortable and evocative of times gone by. The rich colour of the walls works particularly well with the dark wood kitchen units and terracotta floor. Pretty arrangements of dried flowers and grasses pick up the warm autumnal theme.

▲ A cheerful floral living-room
Some of the most successful schemes combine both warm and cool colours. In this comfortable and colourful family room, the floral upholstery combines warm peaches, oranges and pinks with touches of blues and green. The sand-coloured walls provide the perfect background for the vivid colours of the painting over the mantelpiece and the collection of blue and green china with splashes of red.

What warm colours do

In their brightest manifestations, warm colours are brilliant and exciting, while in their more muted forms they create a sense of richness and warmth. The palest shades – the pinks, peaches and primroses – bring a subtle touch of warmth to any scheme. Warm colours advance towards you while cool colours recede. These qualities are exploited by interior designers. If a room feels big and unfriendly they use a colour from the warm side of the spectrum to draw the walls in to make the room seem smaller and cosier.

Pink and pink-tinted whites

Warm colours are not necessarily bright or strong. Pink, peach, beige, cream, pale yellow and primrose are all warm rather than hot. They are derived from other colours by the addition of white, which has a cooling effect. The palest pastels are essentially pretty colours, the colours of cottage garden flowers – roses, primroses, stocks. These delicate paler shades can be used to create a warm and soothing atmosphere in bathrooms and bedrooms, or to add a subtle warmth to an otherwise cool and elegant living room.

Shades of yellow

Yellow is a cheerful, summery colour ranging from the brilliance of sunflowers and buttercups to buttery yellows, muted ochres and sharp lemons. As with the pinks there are degrees of hotness, with those nearest the primaries being the warmest and those with lots of white or a hint of blue being the coolest. Lemon yellow and greenish yellow, for example, look very cold when compared with the warmer, golden yellows.

Because of the great range of shades available, yellow is an extremely useful colour with many applications in the home. It can be teamed with green and white to create a fresh, spring-like effect

◀ Sunny kitchen

Sunlight streaming into this yellow kitchen gives it a wonderful, glowing quality, but the warmth of primrose as a decorative scheme would make this a welcoming room on the bleakest of winter days. Cupboard mouldings and skirtings picked out in a golden yellow to match the tablecloth and white painted furniture, kitchenware and floor tiles combine to give the room a fresh, spring-like feel.

or it can be used as an accent colour to bring zest to a subdued scheme. A deep yellow ochre, or an old gold would create a dramatic impact in an entrance hall, while a pale primrose could be the basis of an elegant and comfortable living room scheme.

Too much of one thing can be tedious, however, so a combination of warm and cool colours can be used to create interesting but harmonious schemes. Primrose with grey is a particularly pleasing combination. If your living room is large and sunny, you could consider a true, singing yellow and team it with touches of its complementary blue – colours taken from nature, cool summer skies with the warmth of the sun.

In the kitchen you'll find that cool colours work best with pine finishes while peachy colours and soft yellows work well with woods like ash which have a greyish tinge.

Yellow is a glorious colour to wake up to, especially if your room has a southerly or easterly aspect which catches the morning light. Sunlight pouring into a yellow room has a wonderful, glowing quality.

▲ Warm colours with cool touches
In this inviting room warm colours combine with cools to create a harmonious and satisfying effect. The buttery yellow walls and pink curtains and cushions are balanced by the sharp green of the sofa fabric and the cool grey carpet.

▲ A little goes a long way
The primaries are such strong colours that they always attract the eye. This yellow vase draws attention to the cast iron fireplace.

▲ Focus on flowers
An austere room can be cheered by introducing a single splash of warm colour. Here, an arrangement of fruit, hydrangeas and anemones creates an interesting and colourful feast for the eye which will brighten a dark corner.

Rich, floral pinks

Pink is an extremely varied and useful colour, ranging from the palest almost-whites through to warm rosy tints. Pale pinks are lovely for bedrooms: soothing yet warm, they combine cosiness with a frivolous prettiness. In the country bedroom they are most often used in combination with floral and sprigged wallpapers and furnishing fabrics.

The particular shade of pink you use will depend on how much, and what kind of light the room gets. A south-facing room with big windows can take a pale, cool pink with a hint of blue; while a north-facing attic room with small windows will need a warmer carnation pink. A pink'that looks bright and cheerful in sunlight can look dreary and washed out in a cold northern light.

Warming a cool room

If you have used a pale pink on the walls and decide that the room is not warm enough, there are several things you can do. As the window is the light source for much of the time, choosing a warm colour for the curtains will flood the room with warm light.

If your existing curtains are in a cool colour, warm them up with a trim in a warm colour. Used along the leading edge of the curtains it will be seen against the light bringing a warm note into the room. After dark, strong, warm colours used for lampshades will bring a rich glow to the room and as a final touch, rugs and cushions in warm tones can be scattered about.

▼ Roses and peonies
The pale and deep pinks are teamed with cool greens in this exuberant floral wallpaper. The deep pink is picked up in a restrained stripe to create a sophisticated dining room.

Sea and sky colours

Along the shores of the Mediterranean white-washed houses sparkle in the sun, their doors and window frames picked out in intense blue or turquoise. Blues, greens and bluey-greens combined with white are the main decorative colours, both inside and out. Their coolness provides a welcome contrast to the heat of the sun.

In cooler climates cool colours must be used with care. Sharp whites and blues can look garish in a pale northern light, but a bluey white, or a broken, pearly grey will look wonderful.

Sea and sky colours vary in coolness, with most blues and turquoises being fairly cold, but with greens and purples ranging from cold to almost warm. Those at the warm end of the purple spectrum contain a lot of red, while warm greens contain either red or ochre. Look at a paint manufacturer's colour chart swatch to see where you would draw the line between the warms and cools.

▼ **Cool and sophisticated**
Blues, greens, turquoise and certain purples are described as cool colours. In nature these are the colours of sea and sky, bluebells and grass, shady woodland walks and heather-covered hills. In your home, they will make your rooms appear larger and cooler: you can use them to create a tranquil effect in a busy living room, or kitchen, or simply to balance a room where warm colours predominate.

The qualities of cool colours

Cool colours appear to move away from the viewer. For example, if a block of red paint and a block of blue paint are placed side by side, the blue will seem to be further away. This characteristic can be exploited to make a small room seem larger and airier. If you have a living room which is smaller than you would wish, consider using shades of blue or green to 'push back' the walls.

However, the need to make a room look larger has to be balanced with other factors, such as the aspect of the room. If your room faces north, painting it a strong shade of blue will make it seem very cold, so you could try a paler shade of blue or green and add dashes of a warm colour elsewhere in the room. Yellow blinds or curtains would give a sunshine glow to a room with pale blue or green walls. In a south-facing room with lots of light – a room with french windows opening into the garden, for example – you can be bolder in your choice of colour. A good apple green would pick up the freshness of the garden foliage, creating an airy and spacious feeling, while the light flooding in makes the room inviting.

▼ Moody blues
A living room with a very cool feel, created by using related shades of grey, green and blue. Warmth comes from the sunlight filtering through unlined curtains, and from the pink of the cushions and the sofa piping.

◀ Working with blue
A room's colour scheme is often built around one large item – a sofa, for instance, or the existing carpet or a favourite rug – carefully teaming or matching all the other items. With blue, however, you will be surprised at the extraordinary number of shades that will quite happily mix with one another. Here there are blues ranging from the dull navy on the ikat table cloth, to the slaty-blue of the sofa, the delft and prussian blues of the china, cornflower blue on the gingham cushion and the wonderful jewel-like royal blue of the glasses.

◀ A southerly aspect
A room with plenty of light from the south or the west can well afford a cool blue treatment. Here, the ceiling mouldings and french windows are painted the same strong blue as the walls, but the effect is cleverly softened by painting the ceiling a soft shade of pink. Wooden furniture and rich, mahogany-stained floorboards give the room a warm glow.

▶ Pale and pretty
Soft light floods through the net curtains to reveal a delicately pretty room with a pale blue theme. The walls and the Lloyd loom chair are painted in a light grey-blue, while the dhurry is in rather more intense shades of blue and grey. Blue and purple are the dominant colours on the appliquéd table-cloth, and the plant was chosen for its blue flowers. Warm accents are provided by the small vase of sweet peas, and the pinks and reds of the painting.

◀ Bathtime blues
Sea and sky colours seem particularly appropriate in bathrooms, where, teamed with white, they look very fresh and clean. Blue will also make a small bathroom look larger, but before you decorate, check where the natural light comes from; if it is northerly, it will make your bathroom seem cold. Here the clean functional lines of the bathroom suite are softened by pretty swagged curtains, and tiling with a shell motif.

Living with cool colours

People tend to divide into two groups in the decorative schemes they prefer: those that go for the cool, spacious feel of sea and sky colours, and those that prefer the warmer, cosier look of sunrise and sunset. Cool colours are soothing and restrained, elegant and grown-up. They are ideal for living-rooms and studies, rooms in which you work and rooms in which you relax. Fresh cool colours make a kitchen light and airy, but in a bedroom they are used most effectively in a balanced combination with warm colours rather than completely on their own.

▼ Going for green
Make a small bedroom look bigger with light, fresh green walls and ceiling with the woodwork picked out in white. Add lots of warm, pretty details in pink and apricot.

▶ Making a point
Glossy dark greens, like strong reds, make a dramatic impact but they should be used in small amounts. A green jug, candlesticks and a bowl of hyacinths wake up a grey marble slab.

▲ **Kitchen choice** Both blue and green work well with white and these crisp colour combinations look particularly good in kitchens, especially where the cooker and other hardware is white.

▼**Green peace** Pastel shades of green give a bedroom a particularly tranquil, airy feel. Here the green walls and table-cloth are complemented by apricot pastels in the cushions, lampshades and quilted bedspread.

Green alert

We have a strong tendency to associate green, in all its numerous shades, with the outdoors, plant life and the countryside, which makes it a natural contender for inclusion in the country-style home. But, while it is a beautiful and flexible colour it can also be difficult to handle.

The paler shades are fairly safe, and will work in most rooms, but you should take special care with some of the others. Some of the sharp yellowy greens, for instance, can look very acidic, and bright leafy greens, though seductive, should be used in moderation. The vivid green from a pretty floral print can look disastrous on paintwork and walls, though it may well look charming as a bright accent on cushions or tie-backs. If you go for impact and choose a strong, dark green wallpaper for the hall or a study, temper it with rich red oriental-style rugs, or it will have a tendency to look gloomy in daylight.

The easiest and most popular greens are those that have been tempered with a warm colour – these are generally the softer, more muted shades like olive, sage and pale avocado. So use bright and dark greens sparingly, in patterns or as accent colours balanced by other strong colours. And if you naturally incline towards greens, choose paler shades or warmer tones and take care to soften them with their complementary reds and oranges.

Taking the chill off

People generally find it difficult to decide whether a green or a turquoise is cool or warm when they see it on its own – it is much easier to see 'warmness' or 'coolness' if there is something to compare it with. Thus a green room accented with blue will be cool; but if your accent colour comes from the opposite side of the spectrum, it will be transformed into a warm room.

▲ Complementary
Turquoise's complementary colour, a lovely orangey-ochre, brings out all its potential warmth. The beech-coloured pot and the bright cloth make the perfect complement for a turquoise chest.

▼ Autumnal accents
A medium jade green is warmed by lavish autumnal curtains, a theme echoed in the cupboard's darker tones. The bright green duvet cover can take the brighter orange of the cushions.

Pastel colours

These are the colours of ice-cream, sugared almonds and blossoming fruit-trees. They are pale and attractive, bringing to mind the blues, pinks and yellows of old-fashioned cottage-garden flowers like delphiniums, larkspur and lupins. Even the names of the pastel palette are wonderfully evocative – sugar pink, Wedgwood blue, almond green, primrose yellow, apricot and soft turquoise.

These attractive, frivolous colours came into their own in the early eighteenth century when the overblown grandeur of the baroque gave way to the style known as rococo which was fresh, free, airy and elegant.

Favourite colours – often used in striped wallpapers of the period were pale and subtle pastels.

Pastels as a background colour

These are useful background colours – they never jar and can be spiced up with splashes of another colour. They are ideal for large areas like walls or floors when you don't want the colour to dominate, yet you do want to introduce a positive rather than a neutral colour.

Pastels are mixed from white and one of the primary colours (see page 8), which accounts for a slight chalkiness in their appearance. It also means that they look particularly good with white. In bathrooms a combination of pastel blue or pink with white fittings and tiles looks fresh, clean and attractive. For a child's bedroom, sponged, plain or wallpapered walls in primrose yellow can be teamed with a yellow and blue sprigged design on a white background.

Pastels in large quantities, or over large areas, can look rather sugary. Equally, because of their high white content pastels can feel a little cool so warm them with earth colours or muted tones. Instead of putting sugar pink with a pastel green like pistachio, try combining it with sludgy olive and beige – the effect will be much more interesting. Other fresh combinations are Wedgwood blue and ochre, almond green with warm grape and grey-lilac.

▼ Pastel colours
Pastel colours are made by mixing colours with white – red and white become pink, green and white become apple green, yellow and white become primrose.

Pastel patterns

Pastels are often used in patterned wallpapers and fabrics, particularly those with floral motifs. However, on close inspection you'll probably find that there is less pastel in a particular pattern than you thought at first. This is because designers have found that slightly muted versions of colours are actually easier to work with than true pastels. However, these predominantly pale and subtle patterns are well suited to the country look. For instance, used in bedrooms they are restful and easy-on-the-eye, but be careful, because pastels plus frills might be too feminine for most men.

For a child's room try soft voile sheers spotted with pink or pale turquoise, and delicately flowered curtains. Add a deep pink carpet – crushed raspberry – and furniture stained a sea green.

Pastel looks

There are many pastel 'looks'. The first uses large areas of flat colour and teams it with white for a crisp clean look. The second again uses large areas of flat colour but teams the chalky pastel colours with muted tones and uses a variety of 'distressed' and textured finishes, an approach typified by the Scandinavian look. The third way of using pastels combines lots of pastel prints and patterned chintzes to create an attractive, country-cottage look.

One of the prettiest looks derives from the rococo style – it combines light and delicate decoration in soft tones with lots of white and cream, pictures of pink cherubs and floating clouds. This will look attractive in an elegant sitting room, and for a really sophisticated look, add touches of 'antique' gilt, on picture frames and mirrors, for example.

▶ **Playing with pastels**
The palest of pastels in yellow, pink and blue have been used to lighten and brighten this long thin hall. The effect could have been sugary, but the dark red stencilling, and the muted colours of the detailing on the cornices and the ceiling rose give the arrangement the necessary edge.

▼ **Patterns in pastel**
Pastel floral wallpaper, curtains and upholstery fabric teamed with warm pine furniture give the dining room a cosy country look.

White with a hint of . . .

Paint manufacturers have developed a whole range of pastels from almost-white through various pale shades to sweet pea colours. These look wonderful in some parts of the home, however try to avoid filling the whole home with off-whites as they can start to look dull.

Unusual colour combinations

Don't always go for the most predictable colour combinations – try powder pink and pale straw, pale lilac and pale gold. For a faded country house look add touches of distressed gilding on wooden frames, curtain poles, and even to pick out details on woodwork such as architraves or fireplace surrounds.

▲ Childish delights
Pastels have always been firm favourites for decorating young children's rooms; a pink and white candy-striped canopy, a flowered bedspread in baby blue, a handkerchief lampshade in primrose, and pink painted furniture, make this a delightful room for a little girl.

▼ Mature pink
The different shades of pink on the walls and ceiling look wonderfully clean and fresh with white paintwork, white curtains and crisp white linen bedclothes. The black and white fireplace and tiles and the wonderful, but unusual bedside table give the overall scheme emphasis.

Pastels with wood

Pastel shades work well with some woods – but not all. Light woods like new pine and bleached woods can make the whole room look pale with pastel colours – this can be avoided by adding a bright picture or rug. However, this combination of pale wood and pastels can be attractive and appropriate in a young child's bedroom, for example.

Similarly, the combination of limed woods and pastels might be displeasing, if it is found in particularly large quantities, as they both have the same rather chalky look – limed woods look much better with colours which have less white in their make-up, such as terracotta, olive and old gold.

Pastels tend to look wonderful with honey-coloured woods like oak, yew, old pine or natural oiled oak – try them with cool colours like Wedgwood blue or almond green.

Cane and pastel shades are a particularly happy combination giving a light, airy look – with touches of white or cream this is ideal for conservatories or living rooms which lead on to a garden. If you have dark woods like mahogany in your home, select from the warmer side of the pastel palette – go for sugar pinks or try using warm apricots.

Pastels with black

For a really alluring and dramatic Art Deco effect combine pastel shades with black. Try combinations such as primrose or eau-de-nil and black, or pale apricot, cream and black. Add chrome fitments – taps, shelves, towel rails and rings. Choose lacquer black frames for mirrors and picture frames, and add details such as fine black lines on walls and doors. Black or grey marble adds to the Art Deco effect, so think about marble-type worktops.

Pastels for children

When a new baby is expected there is a great temptation to decorate the newcomer's room in 'appropriate', theme wallpapers, with lots of bunnies or teddies in fresh pastel colours which you will want to change as the child grows up. A more economical approach is to use natural fabric and tones which can easily be accessorised and dressed up to suit the child's age.

For a new baby you can create a really attractive room by dressing the window with yards of frothy muslin looped up and tied with lots of ribbons and flowers. Wash walls with a sponged pastel emulsion – this won't cost much and can be changed later. Keep the furniture to light pine or bleached oak, and add china handles decorated with floral motifs – these can be changed to primary colours later to suit a child's developing colour sense. Stained floorboards and cotton rugs will be fine until baby is crawling – then invest in carpet with a small patterned motif – or perhaps carpet tiles which you can replace easily when the inevitable spills happen.

▲ Pastel, neutral and black

A delightful combination for the kitchen is sponged primrose walls, with cupboards and paintwork dragged in a pale grey. These colours are repeated in the sprigged floral curtains and the wallpaper border. Touches of gold on the picture frames make them stand out from the wall. But it's the touches of black in the floor tiles and in the charming fat pig on the cupboard that make the scheme really special.

Earth colours

This rich and spicy palette of colours is mainly derived from naturally occurring pigments and was used by our ancestors before the dawn of recorded time. The very first time a human being made a deliberate mark on a surface it was probably with one of these pigments – a piece of charcoal from the remains of a fire, perhaps, or a lump of chalk or simply a clod of red clay from the cave floor. Our instinctive need to decorate our homes and to record the world around us is magnificently illustrated on the walls of the famous caves of Altamira in Spain and Lascaux in France which date from around 25,000 years ago. Here the artists have depicted bison and other animals with deft, swirling lines, filled in with ochres and browns, and the colours of these naturally occurring pigments are still visible despite the time that has passed since they were first painted.

▲ **Natural origins**
Earth colours are those that derive from natural colour pigments found in clays, and their names come from the regions where they were found – sienna from Tuscany, Naples red, umber from Umbria and so on. They are warm, homely colours, with a strong natural feel.

► **Kitchen chic**
*Warm terracotta floor tiles,
dark oak units and olive
patterned wallpaper work
beautifully with white tiles
and surfaces in the kitchen.*

raw sienna

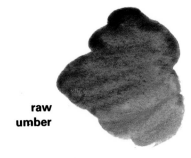

burnt sienna

**raw
umber**

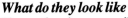

**burnt
umber**

yellow ochre

What do they look like

The earth colours are all on the warm side of the spectrum, ranging from yellow, through various shades of red, brown and green, and including chalky white and charcoal.

They are an important part of the painter's palette, and if you paint you will be familiar with their names which often reflect their place of origin. Raw sienna is a light brown from the hills of Tuscany in Italy. It is the colour of ground cinnamon or nutmeg with distinctly yellow undertones. Burnt sienna, on the other hand, is a reddish brown pigment the colour of ground ginger. The umbers are darker browns originally from Umbria. Raw umber has just a hint of yellow, burnt umber is a dark reddish brown.

The earth yellows are ochres rather than bright yellow, at their brightest the colour of English mustard, but usually more muted – like French mustard. If natural yellow ochres are heated, they produce reddish pigments. This has happened naturally in volcanic regions giving some particularly strong and beautiful pigments such as Naples red from the slopes of Vesuvius.

Of the greens, terre verte is an strong, transparent, true earth green, but for decorating purposes drab and olive greens seem to work best.

Qualities of earth colours

The earth colours are much beloved of decorators. First and foremost they are extremely beautiful colours – warm and subtle rather than brilliant, the colours of autumn leaves and oriental spices. They are almost all in the same tonal range, which means that they can be used together with ease to create interesting and satisfying harmonies. Tone describes the lightness or darkness of a colour. Colours which have the same value or intensity tend to produce a balanced, rather quiet relationship, which is useful if you want to give a room a restful or sophisticated feel, or even if you want a foil for other, more dramatic accents.

Earth colours can be mixed with white to create subtle muted shades which are pretty and extremely useful. Individual tastes vary, but some colours can be recognised as 'good' decorating colours – they are used again and again, and always seem to work. Often these colours are slightly off or 'dirty' colours, giving them a mellow or distressed quality. Earth colours fall into this category as they are full of natural impurities.

Look at old paintings, and see how artists use earth colours to bring a blue scene into warm focus, or to 'anchor' a cream or pink one.

▲ A warm glow
Red and white paper can look pink and washy; here it is enhanced by the dark stairs and a terracotta floor. White lace adds a crisp accent.

▼ Earthy tints
A touch of ochre and sienna on the walls and woodwork make the perfect bedroom background.

Using earth colours

Earth colours are ideal for the country look – they have the functional, no-nonsense, rather puritan feel that goes with natural materials and chunky textures. They can be used to create a rustic look, but they can also look elegant and understated in the right setting teamed with antique furniture.

Earth colours with white

Earth colours look best if a contrast of tone or colour is introduced into the scheme. White, either a brilliant white, or a creamy white, set them off wonderfully. In a bedroom, for example, putty coloured walls would look wonderful teamed with white woodwork and white lace on the bed.

Dark brown or burnt sienna set off by white looks particularly smart. A kitchen floor of terracotta tiles and natural wood units will look fresh and functional with white tiled or painted walls.

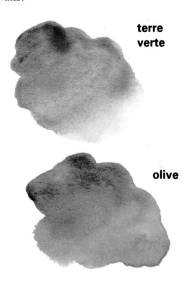

terre verte

olive

▲ Earthenware
The warm natural colours of pottery and earthenware are perfect against the unpainted brick and warm wood of this country kitchen.

◄ Accent blue
The lovely subdued earthy colours in this dining room are beautifully balanced by the splashes of a rich, autumn beech leaf orange, and a faded, chalky blue.

Ochres with cools

The yellow earth colours also benefit from being teamed with cool shades. Try yellow ochre with Chinese blue – an elegant and subtle version of the Provençal combination of bright blue and yellow. For a particularly pleasing colour scheme, use the restful blues for the furniture, with touches of honey tones for warmth. Use pale yellow ochres for the light sources – for lampshades and window treatments – and bring them all together in Chinese rug in delft blue and ochre on a cream background.

Ochres with browns

Walls painted in a yellow putty shade are traditional in the English country farmhouse. Teamed with polished wood, slate, earthenware and richly coloured rugs it combines to create a restful scheme into which accent colours such as a bright golden yellow can be introduced.

◄ Mellow harmonies
A perfect demonstration on how well the earth colours can be used together – stone flagged floor, parchment-coloured walls, stencils in sepia and tan, and an old Persian rug in brick red and dark brown.

Brown earths with cool colours

In design, contrasts often balance a scheme. For this reason, warm colours benefit from the introduction of a cool colour and vice versa.

A cool blue-grey is a useful foil for rich reddish browns. A room with rich, earth-coloured soft furnishings will benefit from cool grey walls. Alternatively, warm brown walls will need lightening with an accent colour such as pale china blue.

In a sitting room try a grey sofa piled high with ochre and russet cushions, with an Indian carpet on the floor echoing all three colours.

In a kitchen terracotta teams well with slate grey and pale blue-grey paintwork.

In the dining room you can afford to go for a more drama than elsewhere in the home. For a really sumptuous effect, try rich rust and brown print curtains and upholstery, a russet tablecloth and a Tiffany shade in a similar range of colours. Finally add wooden Venetian blinds, a polished wood floor and furniture in mellow old woods. Earth colours can be rather dark, so make sure there are plenty of warm pools of light.

▲ *Balancing tricks* This salmon pink coloured wallpaper needs the blue and white flowers to balance its warmth; there are further cooling touches of blue in the carpet, cushions and lamp, the touches of wood enhance the overall effect.

◄ *Bedroom bliss*
This cool grey bedroom with its stripped floorboards is brought to life by the earthy colours of the bed linen in onion-skin red, olive, cinnamon and teal.

▲ *Cinnamon and slate*
This spicy gingery cinnamon, balanced with touches of slate blue is perfect for kitchen tiles, a lovely background for wood, glass and earthenware accessories.

A touch of luxury

Earth colours blend particularly well with natural wood tones, and with other natural materials like cane and raffia, sisal matting, stone and slate. The rather plain and functional feel of these materials and colours provides a wonderful foil for a little splash of unexpected luxury. So why not try white lace curtains inside chunky tweed drapes in grey and brown. Or create a simple but dramatic effect by enlivening a basically rather plain bedroom – grey walls and a rich brown carpet – with lots of white frilly bed linen.

The classic plainness of the background suits traditional furniture in dark woods but because these earth colours have a solid feel, you can also afford to indulge in one or two extravagantly flamboyant touches. For example, in a room in any of the colourways described above you could add an elaborately carved and gilded mirror above the fireplace or gilded wall lights. You'd expect to see lavish accessories such as these against a more obviously opulent colour – crimson, purple, glossy peacock green or blue for example – so the effect is heightened by its unexpectedness.

▲ A touch of gilt
To the simplicity of earth colours, add a splash of luxury with ornate gilded wall lights and a marble bust.

▶ Hearth and home
Warm terracotta walls and an open fire, crowded bookshelves and easy chairs produce an infinitely cosy living room.

▼ Country clutter
Earth colours are very relaxing and easy to live with – colours that encourage reading, sewing and cosy fireside chats.

Natural neutrals

Nature is the richest source of the subtle and infinitely varied shades that make up the neutral palette. From the seashore we can select the pearly pinks and pale ochres of seashells, the muted greys, beiges and softest browns of a pebble beach, or the sparkling whites and yellows of the sandy shore.

Inland we find the warm greys of granite, the bluer greys of slate and limestone, and the buffs, and beiges of sandstones. From field and hedgerow we can take the tawny shades of straw and sun-bleached grasses, autumn leaves and sawn wood.

Technically, neutrals are the shades without colour: black, white and all the greys. To these, interior designers have added beiges, fawns, taupe, stone, putty, biscuit, sand, camel, buff, mushroom, khaki – a myriad of evocatively-named subtle shades almost exclusively drawn from the colours of nature.

Neutrals have two outstanding characterics – they can be used together to create satisfying and harmonious relationships, and they can also be used with strong colours from other groups without creating a clash.

▲ Natural harmony
The great charm of neutral colours is their compatibility with each other and with virtually all the other colours. They make quiet, undemanding backgrounds for bright primaries, or rich berry colours, or cool blues and earthy browns. Used on their own, or accented with grey or black, they look costly and uncluttered.

Neutrals: the total look

An easy-to-achieve interpretation of the country look combines neutral tones with richly textured surfaces. The style is relaxed and timeless, yet capable of endless variety and modification. It is seen in the whitewashed walls, flagstone floors and bleached deal dressers of the traditional English farmhouse. The undecorated simplicity of the Shaker homes of colonial America owed their charm to a combination of natural materials and muted colours.

To achieve this look select colours for walls, floors and soft furnishings from the neutral palette. Combine these colours with natural materials and crunchy textures.

Texture on walls

Different surfaces reflect light in different ways. This characteristic can be used to introduce variety to an otherwise restrained colour scheme. Think, for example, of the difference between matt, eggshell and gloss white paint and exploit these different textures in your neutral decorative scheme. In older homes, plaster can be roughly applied to add textural interest.

The word 'texture' has two meanings in the decorative context. On the one hand it is used to describe the 'feel' of a surface – the difference between the feel of smooth marble, for example, and of rough, unpolished granite.

On the other hand, the word also describes a visual quality – the difference between a plain undecorated surface such as a wall painted in matt emulsion, and a wall that is wallpapered or painted in some way that breaks up the surface – by ragging or dragging, for instance. Wood has texture in both senses of the word because it is rough to the feel and also has a grain which the eye can see. Take advantage of the difference in graining and colour in various woods.

▲ Of bread and baskets
The rustic look in this cottage living room comes from the natural colours and textures of the materials used. Cream painted wood panelling, unpolished quarry tiles, old lace at the windows combine effortlessly with the cane furniture and corn and bread wall decorations.

▶ Textural interest
The natural glow of polished cane and wicker comes into its own set against a neutral background of ivory walls and slightly darker paintwork.

Adding visual texture to your walls can be done in numerous ways. Choose wallpapers in subtle muted shades and smallish patterns like sprigs, florals and mini-prints – the patterns should give textural interest without dominating the scheme.

Paint can be applied to walls and woodwork using one of the many paint techniques so popular at the moment. The simplest techniques, like sponging, ragging and dragging are remarkably quick, easy and effective, even for the inexperienced decorator. The most successful results rely on an eye for clever colour combinations, plus confident handling of paint and materials, rather than knowledge of techniques.

▶ *Full of feeling*
This bathroom relies on texture for its interest. The rough plastered walls are washed with off-white paint; the cupboard has been stripped and bleached to the colour of driftwood. Rough coir matting floor, and woven curtains at the window, white lace hand towels, shells, and a wicker basket, all add more texture to the room.

▲ *Shades of white The charm of this cottage bedroom lies in the many textures in the room. Note the rough plastered walls, the lace curtains, the nobbly rug, the gloss painted floor, the elaborately worked bedspread and the cane chair.*

▲ *Neutral continuity Colour continuity throughout the house will automatically make the place seem larger. But that doesn't mean you have to paint every wall in the same colour. Choose wallpapers with small patterns with backgrounds in similar neutral shades, and you should find that you can easily create visual continuity without tedium.*

Texture on floors

Any natural or textured floor covering works well as part of a neutral country scheme. Plain wood floors can be varnished, waxed, stained, colour washed or stencilled to make them more interesting. If you opt for fitted carpets, select from the stronger neutral shades, and choose rough, tweedy finishes. Any of the natural sisal, coir or seagrass materials will also add texture and warm country colour. These traditional materials are available in a range of patterns, colours and weaves.

Textiles with texture

There are many interestingly textured fabrics available in neutral shades.

Creamy muslin is ideal for unlined curtains, Austrian blinds or festoons which can be used to obscure or dress windows. It can also be used to drape beds or dressing tables. Muslin should be washed and shrunk before use – and don't use it in a steamy atmosphere as it will droop and shrivel. Muslin shouldn't be lined, and looks best if you use plenty of fullness. If you want a darker shade, steep the fabric in tea.

Calico can be used for lined or unlined curtains, or for casual drapes over a pole. Use it for bed drapes or valances, or for tablecloths. Heavier weight calico can be used for upholstery. Brighten up the scheme with contrast piping in bright colours or in other neutrals. Again, do beware of shrinkage.

▲ **Country classic**
A traditional English farmhouse look is based on neutral colours and natural textures. Warm red tiles on the floor harmonize effortlessly with cream walls, and the textures of polished pine and mahogany. Richer textures are added with the velvet curtains, the fringed hanging lamp, the Turkish carpet and the rough cotton of the bright tablecloth.

▶ **Beige is beautiful**
The colour scheme in this sitting room is based on a restful sandy beige. Coir matting, cane and wicker, plants and dried corn, and the various upholstery fabrics, which include heavy striped cotton, ticking and corduroy give warmth and textural interest.

Fine linens can be used for curtains, bedlinen or table linen. Heavier linen and linen union can be used for upholstery and is available in pretty prints and patterns. Edge with linen trims – fan edging, braids and fringes. Add old lace for a traditional country look. Linen should be ironed while damp – but don't expect the smooth, creaseless look to last. The 'lived in' look is part of its charm.

Heavy weaves in silk, cotton, linen or wool mixes are ideal for curtains, soft drapes and throws for beds or sofas – try combining different textures.

Ticking is a traditional country fabric. Use it for curtains, roman blinds, roller blinds, tablecloths, bed valances or kitchen chair squabs. Use the heavier weights for upholstery. Add further interest by switching the direction of the stripes.

Wool flannel can be used for a simple, but elegant look. Use it for curtains in a study, boy's room or living room. Keep the curtains smart and tailored with box or pinch pleats, straight pelmets and piping. Avoid frills, gathers and heavy valances.

▼ *Muted kitchen elegance* On their own the creamy beige walls and floor tiles in this kitchen make little statement; teamed with black bentwood chairs, a grey tablecloth, grey and white striped blinds and a grey and cream rug they proclaim a quiet sophistication. Substitute floral blinds, a cane lampshade and pine chairs for a more lively look.

▲ *Minimally country* This is a lovely French interpretation of the country look. The bedroom is decorated in shades of sand and white, warmed slightly by the honey-coloured parquet floor, and accented by the black metal of the table, chair and lamp. Muslin drapes over the bed add a fresh touch and the effect is enhanced by plain windows.

Neutrals with other colours

Neutrals can also be used to great effect with other colours. The neutrals may be the main colour or the background colour. You can, for example, enliven the gentle harmonies of a predominantly neutral look with splashes of accent colour. Alternatively, you can use neutrals to act as a foil for a vivid colour scheme.

Neutrals are easy to work with so it shouldn't be difficult to find colour combinations that please you. Don't always go for the most obvious – experiment.

Greys are easy to use but need to be sparked up. Try primrose as a second colour, with rust as an accent. Or team it with rust and a touch of eau-de-nil (a light greeny-blue).

Cream also benefits from the enlivening effects of colours such as ochre, lilac, pale green and cornflower blue.

Beige can be teamed with pale blue, deep blue or aquamarine, with a touch of blue-grey, black or white for emphasis.

White goes with almost anything, but try delphinium blue, sunny yellow, fresh spring green or pastel pink.

▶ *A natural for florals*
The bleached sand walls and the textures of wood and cane make a perfect background for curtains and cushions in rich colours and bright, glossy green plants.

▲ **Let the sunshine in** *Off-white walls and paintwork, and the stone fireplace provide a quiet foil for the singing yellow of the heavy silk curtains, and the vase of flowers.*

▲ **Neutrals with warm colours** *A warm shade of white on the walls is deepened by deep apricot curtains held back with flowered tiebacks, and the elegant button-back chair in warm terracotta.*

Introducing pattern

Making the right choice of pattern and colour is the key to creating the 'country look'. That doesn't mean the choice is limited – far from it. There are florals and trellises, stripes and checks, leafy designs and mini-prints, and traditional motifs such as paisley and bows. But it is the combinations of colours and patterns that count.

There are two characteristic looks. One is based on a single pattern – usually for upholstery or curtains – combined with plain walls in 'country colours'. Alternatively, several large and small patterns are combined for a rich, cosy, warm feeling. Whichever of these strategies you prefer will depend on your personal taste: some people prefer to work with one or two patterns in a room, others love a rich medley of colour and pattern. Patterned and plain surfaces can be used in many combinations depending on personal taste, the function of the room and the effect you wish to create.

This and the following chapters introduce you to all the patterns, as well as the broad palette of colours that fit into the country style. Dozens of swatches, photographs and diagrams will help you develop an eye for judging how a snippet of fabric will look when it is covering a large area; how a small sample of wallpaper will look when it is up; and how to combine patterns and colours to achieve pleasing effects.

Pattern with plain

The straightforward way of creating a scheme is to start with a pattern in colours that please you and then build the colour scheme for the room around that – choosing plain colours for walls, flooring and other fabrics that match the colours in the pattern. To carry the principle further, plain curtains can be trimmed with the patterned fabric, or a patterned sofa can be edged with a matching plain piping in a toning or accent colour.

A

B

◀ **The starting point** The sofa fabric (**A**) is the basis for this scheme. The soft leafy print is also used for the blind and a cushion.

Plain accent colours – green (**B**) and deep pink (**C**) – are picked out of the pattern for the curtains, lampshade and cushions.

Co-ordinated ranges

Manufacturers' pattern books are full of lovely co-ordinated ranges of patterns for fabrics and wallpapers. For example, many floral wallpapers are designed to team with a mini print, the two papers being linked by colour or motif. The same pattern theme may also be available in furnishing fabrics, bed and table linen, even kitchen accessories, giving limitless mix-and-match opportunities. These co-ordinated ranges give you the confidence to use two or three patterns knowing that they will combine successfully.

The pictures here show how country-style co-ordinates can be handled in different ways to create a welcoming look – light and airy as in the bedroom, or cosy and warm, as in the dining area. The common denominator in both these ranges is a larger design pulled together and combined with a smaller, all-over pattern – much easier on the eye than combining large-scale patterns.

▲ **Co-ordinated bedroom range** A summery bedroom features different but related fabrics, both linked by the same colours and a rosy motif. The small pattern (**A**) is densely packed. The larger floral pattern (**B**) has a more open design. The plain colours (**C**) on the carpet and walls contribute to a restful, all-over effect.

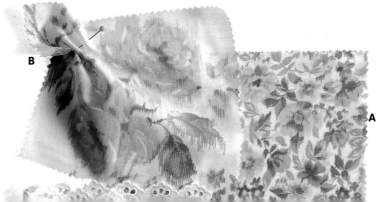

48

▲ **Mix-and-match fabrics** This range shows how well large motifs combine with an all-over design. The tablecloth, napkins, and tea cosy are all made up in the smaller design, while the curtains take up the theme with a larger, posy motif in the same colouring.

◄ **Wallpapers and borders** Flowery sprigs, borders, and an all-over pattern blend to create the total country ambience. (Note how the piping on the cushions picks up the red to provide a plain accent.)

One colour, many patterns

If you enjoy the idea of combining different patterns, but don't want to work with a manufacturer's range of co-ordinates, the simplest approach is to work with a single colour theme. This way you are free to pick up remnants, market bargains or recycle old furnishings. The secret is to settle on one single colour and stick to that. Suppose, for example, that you like pink and that you wish to create a 'pink' bedroom. First, you should choose one item. It might be the bed cover, the curtains or the wallpaper. If you've fallen in love with a floral duvet set in several shades of pink, you might buy curtains in exactly the same fabric, or in another pattern, a

check or a mini-print, but with the same combination of colours.

Next, you might look at the walls. By now you are linking three elements: the bed linen, the window dressing and the wall surface. The easiest and most predictable way forward would be a plain wallpaper or paint in the same sort of pink but matching one of the lighter or darker shades in the pattern. But a more exciting solution would be to find yet another pattern, a stripe for example, in the same colour. Accessories such as china decorations and rugs on the floor can also be included in the colour scheme. By choosing the right combinations, you can bring the comfortable, mellow style of the country house into your own home.

▲ *One colour theme* Here several blue and white florals and checks on wallpapers and fabrics combine to produce a deliciously fresh effect. It doesn't matter if the colours don't match exactly – some can be lighter, some darker. What makes it work is that one basic colour theme is used throughout for walls, cushions and the seat. Even the decorative plates on the wall are blue and white.

Identifying country patterns

There are many different sorts of country-style patterns for fabrics and wallcoverings which group into broad categories. These include florals and mini-prints, spots and stripes, ginghams and checks, as well as traditional designs such as paisley and William Morris. Many of these patterns can be mixed together successfully as later chapters show. Here the patterns that evoke the country style are shown in the form of samples of fabrics and wallpapers.

▲ **Florals and stripes** A traditional floral design – lovely old-fashioned roses and peonies in a bold colourway – teams handsomely with toning stripes. The same mixture of florals and stripes looks just as effective in a paler or cooler colour scheme.

Large florals

These are an important part of the country look. The range of designs is extensive including large splashy watercolour patterns, naturalistic leaves and flowers and stylized designs such as those by William Morris. In some a single colour predominates, in others there are several dominant colours, allowing you freedom in your colour scheme.

Large florals should be handled with care as they can overwhelm in a small room. They are best used for full-length curtains, bedspreads or sofas – but not all at once. In the right context, such as a hall, a rich floral wallpaper can create a warm and welcoming space.

Glazed cottons with colourful designs of flowers and birds are often loosely known as 'chintzes'.

Small all-over florals and leaves

These are available in an abundance of designs and colours. These smaller designs are often well suited to the proportions of contemporary homes. This all-over quality in wallpapers helps to link furniture or furnishings together, and creates a friendly, welcoming feeling in a room.

Sprigs

These are small sprays of flowers or foliage, or even single flowers or leaves, scattered on a plain or subtly textured background. The lighter sprigs are fresh and clean – ideal for bedrooms and bathrooms. Sprigs can seem a bit spotty if there is a lot of plain background between the motifs.

Mini-prints

A mini-print is a very small repeating pattern. It can be any type of pattern including florals and little geometric motifs. Because mini-prints are small they are not overwhelming and when you stand back from them they look more like a textural design. They are useful where you want to introduce a subtle pattern, or in confined spaces such as corridors and cloakrooms. They team successfully with larger patterns, above a picture rail, for example.

Provençal and paisley prints

Originally from the French Mediterranean, Provençal patterns (right) are complex, colourful and often floral. They evolved from imitations of the motifs on Indian cottons, which reached France as exclusive imports in the seventeenth century. In time the Provençal designs became less oriental and more French. Saffron yellow, brilliant red and indigo blue are among the vibrant colours associated with Provençal prints, but they also come in muted, delicate colours.

Paisley patterns (left) are based on the small, familiar Indian teardrop shape. These can be small and neat or large, flowing and filled with flowers to give a distinctly eastern feel to fabrics and wallcoverings.

Textural

These designs are printed to imitate materials such as wood grain and paint effects such as sponging, dragging or spattering. These 'paint effects' are useful where you want to keep your walls simple but not plain. Textural fabrics include cotton damask with its slightly raised surfaces reflecting different light and lace with its more obvious visual texture. Moiré fabrics and wallpapers have a smooth, shiny surface which also reflects light differently in each of the lengthwise directions.

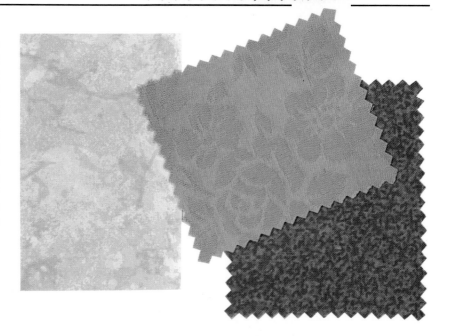

Checks, ginghams and tartans

A check is a pattern of crossed lines forming squares, either woven or printed. Checks can be used on wallpapers, furnishing fabrics and floor coverings. They can be in any colour combination and the effect created depends entirely on the combination of colours. For example, blue and white looks crisp and clean, while a mixture of heathery pastels is gentle and pretty.

Gingham – a cotton material woven from coloured yarns into checks – is a classic fabric that is never out of fashion. The most popular ginghams are red and white or blue and white, though black, green and yellow ginghams can also be found. These are inexpensive fabrics – easy to wash, they always look fresh and clean. Traditionally they are associated with farmhouse kitchens, especially in red and white.

Tartan is a distinctive type of woven check, Celtic in origin, it is created by multiple bands crossing at right angles. The most common tartan materials, such as those used in Scottish kilts, are woven from wool. In the home, tartan patterns have been adapted for use on furnishing fabrics and also wallpapers. Tartan has a timeless quality that never seems to date. Tartan wallpapers tend to be fairly dark and so are best used to give a dining room a cosy quality.

Trellis

These are patterns based on a diagonal lattice or ribbon motif which have a distinctly garden flavour. Sometimes a floral or leafy motif is incorporated, trailing around the trellis. These patterns are usually fresh and clean, ideal for a bedroom, bathroom, hallway or conservatory, or to co-ordinate with floral patterns.

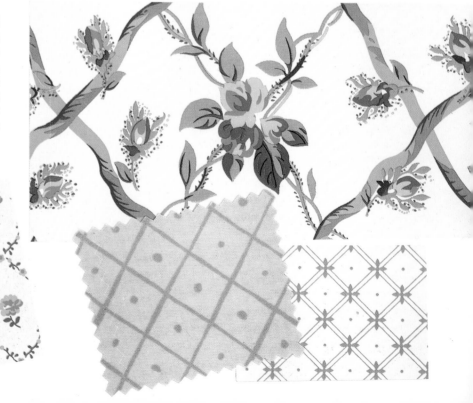

Spots

A popular and traditional pattern which is easy to live with, polka-dots on a white background are bright and cheerful, and work well in small rooms such as bathrooms, kitchens and children's bedrooms. White dots on a coloured background look more grown up, and spotted voiles make charming sheers.

Stripes

Stripes have always been popular, especially for walls and curtains. There are many kinds of stripes – stripes in a single colourway and multi-coloured stripes, broad stripes, narrow stripes and Regency stripes. Candy stripes are narrow, with the white and coloured stripes nearly equal in width.

Country motifs

These tend to be single-colour pictorial patterns. The pictures are inspired by country life and nature: farming and hunting scenes, images of birds, butterflies and plants. William Morris bird patterns fit into this category, as does the French *toile de Jouy*, an unglazed cotton fabric which continues to be made at Jouy outside Paris after 200 years in production.

55

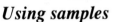

Using samples

When selecting patterned fabric or wallpaper, try at least to get a small sample, about 10cm (4 in) square, to take home. You may find that the colour looks entirely different in natural light or by electric light compared with the strip lights used in the shop.

If you really can't decide if you like a pattern it's a good idea to buy a metre of fabric or a roll of wallpaper, pin it up in the room it is planned for and leave it for a few days. If you don't like the effect you can always use the fabric for cushion covers and the wallpaper for drawer linings.

Better still, allow time to get the shop to order a large sample from the manufacturer for you to take home. You will have to leave a returnable deposit and it may take a few weeks to come, but it's well worth taking the trouble rather than make an expensive mistake.

▲ **Co-ordinating patterns** Small samples can be quite misleading. Here the contrast between the floral and the stripe looks quite strong in the samples. But they blend happily in a larger piece because the colours are gentle and the stripes fairly narrow.

Small florals

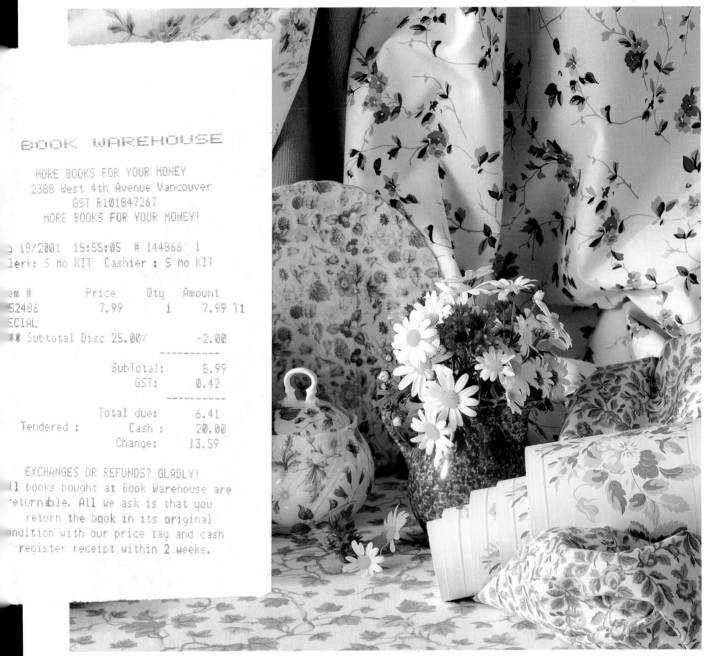

For the country look floral patterns are a key element. They are very popular, and have been so for hundreds of years. This chapter looks at the way small florals can be used as wall coverings, curtain and upholstery fabrics, carpets and accessories.

The term floral is loosely used to describe a wide variety of prints from the familiar cabbage rose designs to leafy prints in a single colour. Yet within each floral category there is a huge range of subjects, styles and colourways. Within the broad category of rose prints, for example, you will find trailing roses, clusters of roses, roses scattered on a

background, roses mixed with other flowers, large roses, botanically correct roses and highly stylized, almost abstract roses.

Small florals are pretty and this is, perhaps, their most obvious quality. It makes them easy to live with and particularly appropriate for the country look. In living rooms bright or pale florals can be used to create a sunny, cheerful feel. Darker patterns can be used to create a richer look, or a cosy, traditional room. The softer, paler small florals look lovely in bedrooms.

In recent years florals have become very popular for co-ordinating ranges,

▲ *A small floral collection A floral design can be interpreted in many ways. The flowers can be stylized, as shown in the fabrics across the top; with leaves and flowers all in one colour as in the blue fabric; an all-over leaf design; or drawn from nature as the decoration used on the china plate and sugar bowl.*

manufacturers offering matching bedlinen, wallpaper, curtains, cushion covers, and sometimes china. The patterns chosen may not, at first, seem to work together but they can be surprisingly successful as shown in the co-ordinated range in the bedroom on page 60.

Choosing florals

Florals can be divided into two g[...]
large and small – and the overa[...]
of these patterns is quite diffe[...]
general big and bold patterns [...]
only be used for large lofty room[...]
patterns – and patterns composed [...]
or closely related colours – work [...]
modern homes, which tend to be s[...]
and have lower ceilings.

Small florals are easier and s[...]
use than large florals. Basically, [...]
patterns, or no pattern at all, make a
room look bigger and are less
overwhelming in today's smaller homes.
If the ceiling height is 2.6m (8ft 6in) or
less, or the room is smaller than 3 x 3.6m
(10 x 12ft), it is easier to use a small
floral pattern than a large one.

Economy is another factor. With
small florals there is less of the waste
involved in matching large-drop
patterned wallpapers.

By choosing a small, all-over floral,
you can unify diverse elements in the
room, such as furniture and decoration.
The pattern complements rather than
fights with the other decorative objects
used in the scheme.

▶ *Florals for upholstery* All-over
designs look inviting and are
practical for upholstery fabrics. This
classic William Morris willow
pattern works well with a range of
country colours such as peach, buff
and blue.

▶ *A matter of scale* The little sample
(above right) looks bright and clear.
The same design seen in a larger
area (right) provides a gentle all-
over pattern that links furniture,
pictures and other decorative
elements.

◀ *Small-scale floral patterns* The
pattern on the tablecloth and curtain
is small enough to enhance, rather
than compete with, the pretty china
and collection of baskets. Note how
the green in the pattern is used for
the door frame.

◄ **Floral floors** Floral prints can also be used on floors. Here a modern carpet design in pale pinks and grey co-ordinates with a flowers-and-stripes wallpaper and spotted drapes. These pale colours and subtle designs introduce a flowery theme while allowing the rich honey tones of old pine to dominate.

▼ **A feast of florals** For this cosy bedroom, a floral pattern in several colourways has been used to warm and pretty effect. The bedlinen, curtain fabric and wallpaper come from a co-ordinated range, but you can achieve this effect by mixing patterns with similar colours and scale. Patterns in rich colours may need to be tempered by neutral areas – like the cream walls and plain floor in this room.

A rich palette

Most floral patterns incorporate several colours, giving you plenty of 'hooks' for your over-all decorating schemes. Some patterns lean towards a particular colour, while others give equal emphasis to several colours. This means that a floral wallpaper is highly adaptable. You can pick out one colour for the carpet and another for the woodwork.

Optical illusions

A pattern is not a fixed thing in the eye of the beholder. Viewed from close-up or in a sample, you may be able to see each flower, each petal, maybe even the stamens of a floral print. But from the middle of the room the same pattern begins to blur and soften. It becomes a pattern of, say, blue and white rather than white flowers against a blue ground.

If the print starts as a soft-edged design against a neutral background, without a great contrast in the colours, the detail dissolves and the eye sees a soft pattern of colours. But if the design is outlined in a dark colour or contrasts strongly with the background, the eye still 'reads' the flowers at a distance.

When you are thinking about pattern in a room, such optical effects are important considerations. Usually people do not want the walls to dominate, they are merely a background to set off the furniture and furnishings to best advantage. So a small pattern with pale colours in similar tones will intrude less than a larger pattern with highly contrasted colours. Strong contrast is best kept for halls and dining rooms where you spend less time; softer, less contrasting patterns for bedrooms and living rooms where you spend more time.

Sprigs

Floral patterns with their suggestion of country lanes and cottage gardens are a delightful way of bringing the countryside into our homes. While the large and small floral patterns discussed in earlier chapters sum up the country look, you'll find that sprigs are actually more popular. Sprigs are not, however, confined to floral motifs – bows, foliage and abstract motifs all come under this grouping. In fact sprigs are quite widespread, once you start looking for them you'll find them everywhere – in magazines, shops and in other people's homes, used on walls, curtains, carpets, tiles and ceramics.

Identifying sprigs
The difference between a sprig and other floral designs is the amount of background which shows between each motif. In a sprigged design the flowers, leaves, twigs or abstract motifs are scattered over the background so that when you stand back and view the pattern from a distance, the overall impression is rather spotty. Individual motifs dance around the wall surface, rather than blending together to create a continuous pattern.

They are popular because they are easy to use and effortless to live with – they allow you to introduce a floral motif without overwhelming the room. The motifs may be naturalistic, simplified or so abstracted that their origins are barely recognizable – the fleur-de-lys is derived from the iris, for example.

The most common type of sprigged pattern has a pale background – often white, sometimes cream. These are fresh and springlike, ideal for small rooms to which they give a bright cottagey feel.

They can also be found with textured, spotted, striped or trellised backgrounds, but these background patterns are subtle with the sprig as the dominant feature.

Different motifs create different effects and you should bear this in mind when selecting wallcoverings or fabric. Carefully rendered sprigs of formal flowers on a pale background look elegant and suit a formal setting such as a living room, or dining room, in a well-proportioned home.

Looser groups of wild flowers suit a less sophisticated setting – for example, bedrooms or living rooms with low ceilings, small windows and a generally rustic feel.

Simple, rather graphic motifs look extremely elegant used as part of a restrained, but pretty decorative scheme in a dining room – this type of pattern offering a compromise between the flowery and the abstract.

▼ Simply sprigs
Although the typical sprigged fabric or paper shows flowers on a plain white or cream background, plenty of other motifs and backgrounds are around – there's certainly a sprig for every occasion.

Sprigs for floors

Sprigged designs are becoming increasingly popular for floor coverings. Plain carpets are undoubtedly very attractive and also provide a useful setting for heavily patterned walls and furnishings, but they do show marks and wear and tear, especially the paler shades. A small, sprigged pattern will act as a camouflage and whilst it will not hide marks, it will distract from them by breaking up the surface. A single stain will jump out of a plain continuous surface, but will not be so apparent on a patterned surface because the eye will move to and fro from one motif to another, rather than lingering at a single point.

Halls and stairways

Because they are light and pretty these patterns are particularly suitable for walls in halls, landings, staircases, lobbies and dark nooks and crannies. They can be used to brighten dark corners and provide a decorative surface without being overwhelming. This is particularly important in a restricted space where the pattern will be seen close to. Sprigged carpets work well in these locations for the same reasons.

Kitchens

Sprigs, especially those on a white background are popular in kitchens because they offer a white surface which looks clean and hygienic, but also pro-

▲ Flowers underfoot
A sprigged carpet looks particularly pretty in a bedroom. Here the motif is in muted shades to complement the walls and curtains.

vide little accents of colour which can be used to tie together a colour scheme. They can either be used on wallpapers or on tiles. In the latter case the patterned tiles may be scattered amongst plain ones, preventing an otherwise plain surface from being too severe. Choose bright primary colours – reds, yellows or blues are good kitchen colours – and team the tiles with checked, striped or plain curtains and kitchen accessories in a co-ordinating colour.

▼ Bright hall
A light, bright, sprigged wallpaper is ideal for cheering up a small hall or lobby with a limited amount of light.

▲ Old world charm
In an old-fashioned, country kitchen a red and white fir tree sprig makes a cheerful background for pine cupboards and lovely traditional, floral curtains.

▲ Sprigged tiles
Sprigged tiles with a bright blue and yellow motif on a white background look fresh and sparky in the kitchen.

63

Bathrooms

Sprigs on a white background are often used in bathrooms for the same reason as they are used in kitchens – the white is associated with cleanliness while the motif adds a touch of colour. Many manufacturers produce ranges of co-ordinating tiles and fabric. For a really pretty effect choose pastel colours; ideally the pattern should incorporate both warm and cool shades – pinks, blues and greens. Tile around the splash-backs, combining plain tiles with patterned ones, and use the sprigged fabric to make Austrian blinds. A plain carpet in one of the pastel shades will add a slab of solid colour.

◄ Pale prettiness
This unusual bedroom has been decorated with fabrics and papers from a co-ordinated range. Sprigs in both the canopy and on the wallpaper are in identical green and yellow, while the canopy background of pale grey moir matches the wallpaper below the dado. Striped jade lining for the canopy, enhances the theme.

Sprigs in the bedroom

Use a pink and green rosebud motif on the walls of a small bedroom. Team it with curtains in the same fabric, or a co-ordinating range, lined with pink to give the room a rosy glow. Choose a crushed raspberry carpet, and plain white bed linen with broderie anglaise frills and details. The cool whites will be balanced by the warm pinks and the sprigs on the

▲ Sprigs and swags
A sprigged fabric in pinks and greens with a co-ordinating wallpaper border is attractively swagged with bows in a matching striped fabric.

◄ Keep it cool
Two frilled, sprigged fabrics in blue, green and white, set against a delicately patterned blue wallpaper, create a restful atmosphere.

walls, and at the window, will hold the whole scheme together.

For another simple bedroom treatment start with a range of sprigged bed linens – there are many to choose from. Match one of the colours in the motif and use that on the walls – applying the paint as a simple colour-wash, or sponge it on. The effect should be subtle, so that the colour is delicate and does not create a distracting pattern. At the windows either use pale curtains in a co-ordinating fabric, or choose plain roller blinds in a neutral colour taken from the pattern – cream or a golden straw colour for example. Natural floor materials would look good – either bare floor-boards, coir or sisal matting. A few rugs in a similar colour range would soften the look. Rich, golden pine furniture would look particularly pretty with this scheme.

Co-ordinating sprigs

Sprigs can be mixed and matched with other patterns, with mini-prints and large florals, for example, and also with plains. Sprigged curtains with a plain lining look very pretty, especially if you turn the lining back when draping the curtains into the tiebacks. Or use a large sprigged motif for cushions, with a smaller design for the frills. There are lots of wallpaper and fabric collections which have mix and match schemes that include large and small sprigs designed to co-ordinate.

Sprigs on a textured background

Small sprigs, widely scattered over a white background, can be distracting if used on a large unbroken surface. Because there is such a strong contrast between the background and the motif the eye jumps from one element to another and never finds anywhere to rest. The closer in tone the motif is to the background, the less this happens, so if, for example, you are going to wallpaper a big room, choose a design which has less background showing, or one in which the background is quite strongly coloured or textured.

There are many patterns which have a light, but textured background – a subtle sponged or marbled effect, for example. Others have a spotted or trellis background pattern. These reduce the contrast between motif and background, making these designs suitable for large rooms where a plain background would not be so effective.

▲▶ **Mixing and matching**
Combining sprigged fabrics and papers with other patterns can be rewarding. Above, a sprigged wallpaper is set above a striped one and a sprigged blind makes a lining for the pretty floral curtains. Right, a harmony of blues is created by using a small sprig with a blue background for tablecloth and curtains, and one with a creamy background for the walls.

Mini-prints

Mini-prints are incredibly versatile and easy to use, and are particularly well suited to country homes, especially those with smaller rooms and lower ceilings. Their popularity goes back to the very early days of printed wallpapers and fabrics in the 18th century. Their scale suited the elegant proportions and restrained decor of contemporary Georgian homes. The early Victorians also favoured the tiny, all-over sprigged designs, usually in darker, richer colours. Towards the end of the 19th century, however, mini-prints dwindled in popularity as the larger, bolder, stylized patterns that we now associate with Liberty prints became the latest craze.

Mini-prints came back into fashion in the 1970s. The trend was spearheaded by Laura Ashley, whose designs were based on 18th century and Indian woodblocks. Laura Ashley designs – tiny repeating motifs and small sprigs – became the rage for wallpapers, furnishing fabrics and high fashion clothes. Laura Ashley's influence was immense, and many of her designs have become classics. Mini-prints seem to have become a permanent part of the design repertoire.

People who had used plain colours throughout the 1960s started to introduce pattern into their homes, they even began to mix patterns: mini-prints with mini-prints and then mini-prints with

Choose from a wide range of mini prints for your country home. They can be used anywhere around the home from tiling to curtains. This selection shows some of the varieties of mini-prints which are available in the shops.

large prints. Manufacturers responded to demand by developing co-ordinated ranges with plains, large prints and mini-prints. Tile manufacturers and carpet manufacturers followed suit with ranges of tiny and sprigged prints.

Choosing patterns and colours

Mini-print wallpapers, fabrics, tiles and floorcoverings are available in a huge range of designs and colourways, so where do you start? If you want to mix patterns there are several ways of finding designs which will go together. The easiest method is to stick to one family of colours, blues, for instance. The pretty

◄ **A cool blue room**
Co-ordinating wallpaper and fabric in a blue foliage print combine attractively with a geometric print in another shade of blue.

blue bedroom on the facing page shows how successful this approach can be. If, however, you want to use more than one colour, find a linking colour which appears in every pattern – it may be the dominant colour in one pattern but only a minor theme in another. When working with large multi-coloured prints select one or two colours from the main print and find a mini-print in these colours. In the room at the bottom of this page a delicate sage green mini-print has been teamed with large florals – it is used above the dado rail and also in the panels below.

◄ **On a pink theme**
Offcuts have been used to make these pretty scatter cushions – pink links the different patterns.

▼ **Large and small**
A subtle green mini-print is teamed with floral curtains and an exuberant rose border.

69

◄ **Strong colour**
This bright sunshine yellow miniprint 'reads' as a single colour from a distance because the background colour is so strong and the dots are close together.

tip

Mixing mini-prints
Take the worry out of mixing patterns and colours by choosing from a fully co-ordinated range of wallpapers, curtain fabrics and bedlinens.

How we see mini-prints

Because they are small, mini-prints tend to 'read' as a single colour when viewed from a distance – in a large room, or down a corridor, for example. Denser patterns will read as a dark shade of the colour, while those with more white background showing will read as pale.

If you intend to use a mini-print on a large surface, stand back from it to see what the overall colour is – it may well be different from the colour which dominates when you look at it close-to. Half-closing your eyes will help you see how it will look.

The way you see a mini-print also depends on the degree of contrast within the pattern. If the colours in the pattern are close in tone they will tend to merge together. If, however, the colours are highly contrasted, blue on a white background for example, the individual motifs will hold their form for a greater distance.

The space between the motifs is also important: if the sprigs are close together they will tend to merge, but if they are widely scattered on a plain background they will be seen as separate elements for a greater distance. If the motifs are both widely spaced and in strong colour contrast to the background they will remain separate even longer – for example, black stars on a white ground will remain distinct, whereas grey stars on a cream background will quickly merge to create a single colour.

Practical uses

Because they are small and dainty, mini-prints will not overwhelm a small room. They are often used very effectively in small bathrooms, bedrooms or hallways, where, teamed with a plain colour, they can make the room feel quite spacious, especially if pale, cool colours are selected.

One great advantage of mini-prints is that the small scale of the patterns means that they are easy to use in those oddly-shaped rooms so characteristic of older homes. A wallpaper with a small pattern and a small repeat can be used where there are sloping ceilings, uneven walls and corners which aren't square. The pattern will hide any unevenness in

◄ **Strong pattern**
By contrast this relatively subtle pattern holds its form at a distance because there is a strong contrast between the widely spaced motifs and the pale background.

the wall surface where a plain colour would show it up.

Small overall patterns also help to break up large areas and, by distracting the eye, camouflage awkward spots. A large pattern with a large repeat is both difficult to match when walls are out of the true and would draw attention to any structural irregularities in the room.

Mini-print designs are also practical for carpets in rooms and hallways that get heavy use, as they tend not to show the dirt in the way that plain carpets do. They can be teamed with plain walls or walls with a small pattern.

On walls you could even take a mini-print up to dado level with a plain colour above.

Checks and ginghams

This large group of traditional patterns is bright, cheerful, easy to use and generally cheap. They appeal in particular to people who prefer a simple, uncluttered interpretation of the country look as a satisfactory way of introducing pattern, texture and colour without using the more obvious florals.

Gingham, madras, prince of wales and hound's-tooth checks are all traditional check patterns. Gingham was always made from a sturdy woven cotton, madras from a much finer, thinner cotton, while prince of wales and hound's-tooth checks were woven wool fabrics. However, modern weaving and printing methods mean that it is now possible to have a hound's-tooth check printed on, say, linen; or a gingham type check in fine wool.

Using checks and ginghams

Checks and ginghams are fresh, crisp and cheerful, and they are an ideal way to capture the simplicity of a rustic country cottage. They can be mixed together on cushions, chair seats and small armchairs. They aren't normally used on large items like sofas as the pattern would look too busy and would be visually disturbing. However, there are exceptions to every rule and in a room with a lot of strong flat colours a gingham sofa can look dramatic. Checks and ginghams can also be used for curtains, and for small items such as table cloths and lampshades.

Checked fabrics and wallpapers can be used to brighten up a plain room or as the same way as can be done with floral patterns (see pages 57–60). They can also be used in a single-colour room – combining green and white checks with green walls and white woodwork, for example. Finally you can, with care, mix a selection of checks of different sizes – and even different colours – together to create a bright, rather jolly effect. This would be fun in a children's room, a family room or a kitchen.

◄ **A checked collection**
The traditional gingham check comes in a range of sizes and colours, each fabric using a single colour with white. Checked patterns are equally diverse in size and they can also introduce two, three or more colours into the pattern.

Checks in the kitchen

Checks and ginghams which combine white with one other colour look particularly good in kitchens and kitchen diners. Patterns containing a large proportion of white always look fresh and clean, a quality we instinctively seek in a room where food is prepared. The white in the pattern also works well with white enamelled and glazed surfaces, the traditional finishes for sinks, tiles and stoves. These days electrical goods such as cookers, dishwashers and fridges are available in a whole range of colours, but fashion is very fickle and you may find you tire of brown or red kitchen equipment, while white never goes out of fashion.

Checks and ginghams look particularly attractive with the woods used for traditional kitchen furniture – pine, oak and beech, but they also work well with darker woods.

The use of checks with plain washed walls, bare wooden floors and country furniture can be traced back to cottage interiors of the past. This image of the typical cosy country kitchen has been kept alive in many ways, particularly in the illustrations in traditional children's books. They have re-appeared in recent years in television advertisements for products that the manufacturers wish us to associate with traditional values – with naturalness and wholesomeness.

The reason for the historic popularity of these cotton materials was above all practicality; they were tough, easy to wash, and cheap. This country style can also be seen in French provincial homes and in another form in the interiors of American colonial homes. In the American interpretation of the style, checked fabrics were often combined with naturally darker woods or dark wood finishes. All these styles have a long history and have never entirely dropped out of fashion.

Checks for a quick lift

Checks are simple patterns, but they nevertheless have an impact which is out of all proportion to the amount of the pattern used. Even in a room full of patterns, checks and ginghams will stand out because of the simple geometry of the design motif – repeating squares, straight lines and right angles – which the eye can read and retain very easily. Stripes also have this quality.

Less geometric designs such as florals are more complex, and less direct. So a small floral will tend to merge into the background, whereas a check on the same scale will demand attention. Floral and other asymmetrical patterns rely on colour and scale for their impact. For

▲Kitchen charm
This very simple white-walled country kitchen is taken out of the ordinary by its cheerful gingham curtains, blue and white china and the bright splashes of red in flowers and pepperpots.

◄ Mix and match
You need to be bold to use a check on a large piece of furniture – but it works beautifully, teaming confidently with the blue and white patterns on the walls, curtains and lampshade and china.

▶ Checks for impact
A checked curtain in warm
shades of russet, olive and
cream hung across the
garden door gives a
warm, dramatic glow to
the hall, which is
otherwise simply
decorated in matching
shades.

this reason checks can be used to give a quick, inexpensive lift to the way a room feels – the most appropriate applications, however, are in the kitchen. Choose a predominant colour, it might be a red floor, or even red trims and knobs on built-in units, and find a fabric that matches. Use it to make cottage-style curtains tied back with bows. Make up some flat squab cushions for your kitchen chairs, finishing them off with bows.

Finally, you can use the same fabric to make a table cloth and a few small items such as oven mitts, tea cloths and perhaps a tea cosy or apron. You will find that you have achieved a transformation and given your kitchen a new lease of life for very little expenditure of either time or effort.

Checks for children
Checks and ginghams are ideal for children's rooms, where bright, stimulating colours and cheap but hardwearing materials are essential. Brilliant primary reds and blues work well, but any combination of strong clear colours will look equally good. The checks can be combined with patterns designed for children – these are sometimes based on motifs such as trains, cars, toys or on

their favourite story book characters. Their simple flat colours on plain, often white, backgrounds team easily with checks or plains in bright colours.

Blue and white
Of all the colours used in the country home, the combination of blue and white is the most popular and persistent. This is particularly reflected in the ranges of blue and white chinaware and tiles, in designs derived from almost every part of the world and every period of history – think of delft tiles, and the willow pattern. Similarly, blue and white gingham is ever popular – and can be used creatively in any kitchen to suggest that country look, especially if you already have a collection of blue and white china.

Large and small checks
Many fabric companies produce the same check in large or small versions. This gives you a great deal of flexibility in devising treatments for soft furnishings. You could, for example, use a large check for curtains or roman blinds, and a smaller version for cushions, chairs and tablecloths. You can even use large and small checks on the same item. Use the small check to make a border and tie-backs for curtains in a large check,

▲*Checking it up*
This room cleverly combines different types of blue and white checks – on the bed curtains, the valance and the wallpaper – with blue and white striped sheeting and an abstract patterned rug. The surprise is the floor, stained in checks of warm brown and the natural wood.

▲Floor check
An Edwardian tiled hall floor strikingly mixes squared patterns with diagonal patterns in a rich yet subtle combination of rust, black, grey and cream, mellowed with age.

▼Sitting ducks
The bright primary colours of the sunny check wallpaper and the great bowls of scarlet pelargoniums make this old fashioned, stone-floored sitting room seem very warm and welcoming.

▲Chequerboard
One of the oldest floor designs in the world must be the black and white chequerboard, set here on the diagonal. The design is popular in halls and kitchens, and can be done in tiles, lino or painted wood.

▲Cheerful china
Perk up a modern, streamlined kitchen with rustic plates in bold blue and white checks.

◄ Bathroom tiles
Tiny check tiles make a welcome break for the eye in a blue and yellow floral bathroom.

▼Childish checks
A dream bedroom for a little girl teams floral curtains with wallpaper in tiny pink and white checks, with matching larger checks for the mirror frame and dressing table curtain.

then use the large check to make a border for the small check tablecloth.

Lining up
Checks and ginghams can be used straight-on or on the diagonal. Cut the fabric on the diagonal to add interest to the borders, cushions or tie-backs. Experiment to see what happens when you gather the check in one direction – the horizontal lines along the gather show more strongly as the vertical lines disappear into the folds. Use this phenomenon for shirred tie-backs or for a ruched band at the top of a valance.

Trellis

Trellis patterns in all their forms are a useful addition to the collection of country motifs. In its simplest form trellis consists of a basic geometric diamond or lattice-work pattern, usually drawn with thin lines on a plain, pale background. On wallpaper and furnishing fabrics, however, trellis is often combined with a floral motif, either sprigs scattered within the rectangles, or with floral or leafy motifs twining around the basic geometric structure. It is also a popular design woven in self-coloured, textured fabrics like damask, jacquard or cotton twill.

Trellis patterns may be large or small, simple or complicated, but apart from a few rather severe or violently coloured designs they are almost always appropriate in a country style home.

▲ Trellis variety
Just a few of the immense variety of trellis patterns: trellis with a formal flower design inside the diamond; a mini-print trellis; a trellis with a large floral superimposed on it, and, on the table, a double trellis with a floral motif.

▲ Cane, pine and bamboo
A green bamboo trellis wallpaper is used to great effect in a hall with stripped pine doors and an interesting bamboo display cabinet. The wildflower curtain fabric adds vital touches of scarlet and mustard to the scheme.

◄ Basic style
A really simple trellis pattern can be used as a neutral background: here it works as a restful complement to floral curtains, a mini-print blind and some rather exotic cane furniture.

Types of trellis pattern

Basic lattice pattern These simple geometric patterns – a line against a pale background – are particularly useful in situations where you want to introduce a bit of surface interest and colour, but retain a formal feel. In a basically neutral room a creamy wallpaper with a trellis motif in a pale ochre would add a touch of colour and texture so subtle that it would only become apparent on close inspection. A pale, widely spaced stripe would have a similar effect, but stripes seem grand and formal, whereas a trellis suggests the controlled informality of a well-managed garden.

Bold contrasts Be careful how you use plain, wide trellis in a dark colour against a pale background or the other way around. On their own on a large surface they can set up disturbing visual effects, so only use them in a room in which the wall surface will be broken up by furniture, shelving and paintings, or above a dado, perhaps rather than on a mass of wall.

Implied trellis In some patterns the trellis is implied rather than drawn, so the design forms are organised in repeating diamond shapes, but the actual trellis is missing. Nevertheless, the eye interprets the pattern as a trellis.

Double trellis Another variation on the trellis motif are the double trellis patterns in which the straight lines are duplicated. There are also various kinds of basket-weave designs, generally found in brown and green colours, which have a distinctly rustic feel like real trellis.

▼ Garden illusion
Designed to give the effect of nailed white garden trellis, this paper creates a striking background for a garden room complete with cane furniture and trailing plants.

▲ Implied trellis
The trellis pattern in this deep glowing paper is actually formed by the spaces between the motifs. Its rich colours give the room a high Victorian feel.

Trellis with floral or leafy motifs

These trellis patterns are a happy combination of floral or leafy patterns, with an underlying geometric structure that holds them together and gives them a more formal feel.

The patterns may be large or small scale, simple or complicated. Generally they are on a white or light background which gives the pattern a light and airy feel. The scale of the pattern should be chosen for the space in which it will be seen – a large open trellis would work in a large room but not in a narrow hallway. A small trellis on the other hand will look like a small floral when seen at a distance in a large room.

The trellis can be big, bold and quite ornate with curls and twirls like wrought iron grills. This could well be the dominant feature of the room, and should be used with care, for curtains perhaps, using plainer patterns elsewhere in the room.

All the climbing plants have been used as trellis motifs at some time, either in a natural form or in a simpler, more abstract interpretation. The most popular is the rose, followed by ivy, but wisteria, passion-flower and honeysuckle feature too. Sometimes the trellis is lightly scattered with plant tendrils, sometimes they are massed so that the framework is obscured by the buds, leaves and flower heads.

In some particularly pretty forms of the pattern the diamond-shaped structure is provided by loops of ribbon, with exuberant swags of flowers dotted about, either at the intersections or in the centre of the spaces. Other popular trellis patterns can be made up with bamboo and cane which give the room a slightly oriental flavour.

▲ The cottage look
A very pretty and informal version of trellis in primrose, blue and green looks charming in a cottage living room with pine furniture, baskets and rustic trappings.

▼ Hothouse trellis
A deep-diamond trellis, patterned with luxuriant foliage, gives an exotic planthouse feel to a bathroom rich in hanging baskets and interesting ornaments.

Ways of using trellis

Floral or leafy trellis patterns are a lovely way of introducing a light, bright, spring-like feel into a room. It works particularly well in living rooms, especially those which connect directly to the garden or a conservatory where the suggestion of garden architecture would be particularly appropriate. They can also look very pretty in bedrooms.

The lozenge form of the trellis pattern is a useful device, because you can use it to modify the optical proportions of a room. If the ceilings are low, consider using a trellis pattern to give it height. To do this effectively the pattern should be taller than it is broad and the pattern small enough to allow plenty of repeats between floor and ceiling. It can also be used to give width – to a short wall at the end of a hall for example. In that case the lozenges should be wider than they are high.

The size of a trellis pattern is an important factor in the way in which it is used. Very small patterns are useful as co-ordinating patterns which can be used as a contrast to more eye-catching designs, providing a subtle contrast which is neither plain nor boring. A wallpaper with a small trellis and flower motif could, for example, be teamed with curtains and furnishings in a large floral design.

A wallpaper in a larger pattern would work well teamed with a splash of a good strong colour – in curtains for example. Remember that if you do choose a large scale pattern you must allow enough for matching the repeats which may make decorating a room expensive.

The background in most trellis patterns is pale, and the contrast between the motif and the background holds the pattern even at quite small sizes. This means that most trellis patterns are strong and will 'read' even when the trellis itself is quite small and seen at a distance. The greater the contrast the more the pattern holds.

▼ **Large and small**
This leaf trellis looks clean and fresh on two sizes of glazed tiles.

▶ **Summer bower**
A wildflower trellis gives the sitting room a year-round summer feel.

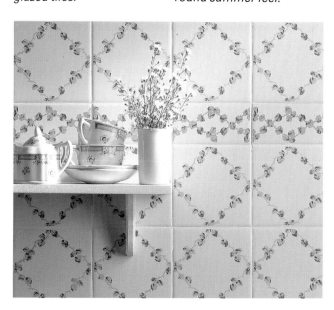

▼ **Leaves and flowers** *A wallpaper version of the leaf trellis shown above is echoed here by the floral tablecloth.*

▲ Touches of trellis
A formal country bedroom has a green and cream trellis carpet, an interesting Chinese lacquer work chest with a trellis front, and a black and gold trellis lampshade.

▲ Trellis with frills
Exuberant flowers and frills rampage over trellis patterned bed-linen.

▼ Country trellis
This trellis pattern on the curtains will only be apparent when drawn.

Trellis on furnishings
If the background is a more definite colour, there will be less contrast between the motif and the background, making the pattern less visually busy. This type of trellis is particularly useful on furnishings where a large, contrasting pattern can be very distracting. You'll also find that on furnishing fabrics with pale backgrounds the floral motif wanders across the spaces between the trellis, another device which breaks up the spaces and makes them less distracting.

Be careful when matching patterns and allow for the extra material you will need to get it right. A badly matched trellis or diamond pattern will look dreadful if the apex of the diamond runs unevenly along the top of curtains, for example.

The more elaborate designs are best used in small quantities in situations which show off the design – perhaps on a roller blind, or for dramatic effect on a hall wall.

Diamond, double diamond and trellis patterns are traditional patterns for quilted bedspreads, particularly in Italian quilting, a decorative form of corded quilting.

Stripes

From the simplicity of ticking to the sophistication of Regency, stripes offer the decorator plenty of styles, designs and colourways to choose from. Slender and restrained, or big and bold, the stripes may be alone or combined with a pattern, and they may be alternated with floral motifs, or decorated with entwined foliage and flowers for a very fresh country look.

Stripes are not only very varied, but they are also extremely versatile. They can be used horizontally or vertically to enhance or restrain the proportions of a room by making it look taller or wider, or used on the diagonal to create unusual borders or trimmings for other fabrics. They can enhance other plain or patterned fabrics, and add depth without rivalling the other designs used.

▲ **Striped variations**
There are many ways in which stripes are used in fabrics and wallpapers: they may be vertical or horizontal, broad or narrow, monochrome or multi-coloured, and they may be combined with other patterns or motifs, for a wealth of styles and effects.

▲ Bright delight
A printed fabric with wide, multi-coloured stripes and bold, floral motifs, makes a bright and cheerful curtain. The fabric is so eye-catching that an ornate curtain style is not required.

▼ Elegant option
In contrast to the picture above, the stripes here are designed to be very subtle, adding interest to the walls and linking the colours of the curtains with the bedding and paintwork.

Printed, woven or embossed?

On wallpapers, stripes may be printed, or they may be embossed in order to achieve a self-coloured effect – sometimes a combination of both is used to give the design depth and interest. Stripes are also printed on to fabrics, or they may be woven, either in a self-colour with a difference in texture defining the stripe, in a contrast colour, or a combination of both.

The dyed yarn in woven designs becomes an integral part of the cloth, so these fabrics often have more texture and depth of colour than printed fabrics, where the dye sits on the surface of the cloth. This is not always the case, however, and many printed fabrics have incredibly vivid and intense colours. Texture is obviously an important element in self-coloured textiles in which the stripes are created by changes of weave and texture.

Printed stripes tend to be smoother than woven stripes as the dye 'takes' better on an even surface. Sometimes stripes are printed on to a textured fabric to deliberately exploit the way the uneven surface breaks up and softens the printed design.

Playing tricks with stripes

There are all sorts of ways in which you can deceive the eye with colour and pattern – stripes, for example, can be used to modify the appearance of a room. Thin, vertical stripes emphasize height rather than width and can therefore make a room look taller. Narrow stripes can be used to draw attention to a particularly tall window, or, if you find the height excessive, wide stripes can be used to make it look less tall.

Horizontal stripes, provided by border wallpapers, or even strongly linear devices like dado rails and picture rails,

make a tall room seem broader by drawing attention to the wall-to-wall dimension rather than the height.

Working with stripes

Stripes are most easy to use on flat, rectangular surfaces, so that you avoid the problems associated with working straight lines round irregular shapes and surfaces, creating odd joins and converging lines – flat blinds like roller blinds and Roman blinds are therefore an ideal application. In either case a striped fabric works well without any further embellishment.

If you want to add interest to striped blinds, you can play with their linear qualities. On a Roman blind, for example, you can make a border in a plain contrasting material, or you can use the same stripes at right angles, or even a stripe in a contrasting colour.

When heading curtains with pinch or

goblet pleats, it is usually possible to make the pleats follow the pattern of the stripes – spend some time working out how the stripes will fall before you finish the side seams so that you can make adjustments to the width if necessary. One of the joys of these cheaper fabrics is that you can afford to be lavish with quantities – use two or even two and a half times the width of the curtain track or pole and make the curtains longer by about 5cm (2in) so that they cascade on to the floor.

Stripes can be used on soft furnishings, but be careful as there will be a lot of wastage with certain kinds of patterns. Choose very narrow or simple stripes in which the matching problems are minimal, or wider stripes overlaid with a tracery of floral motifs, so that the underlying stripes are partially masked, again avoiding too obvious mismatches of repeats.

Use stripes as piping, binding, borders and frills for all sorts of soft furnishings, as a contrast to plain or spotted fabrics. For cushions that combine stripes and florals, place a floral motif in the centre of the cushion cover and make a mitred frame in a matching striped fabric. Striped fabrics also work well for the whole cushion, particularly in one colour plus white which is very fresh and clean when combined with floral or plain fabrics and furnishings.

You could have fun in the kitchen by teaming red and white spots with stripes. Trim a spotted cushion with piping and a 2.5cm (1in) striped frill. Curtains in the same spotted fabric can also be trimmed with a 2.5cm (1in) border of the same, and the striped fabric can be used to make bow tiebacks. The effect is fresh, jolly and very country.

Striped rugs and runners are useful for bringing the flooring into a room's decorative scheme, by picking out the colours of the main flooring and those of the walls or

◄ Refreshing stripe
A stripe of one colour plus white, makes a fresh and appealing Austrian blind, and the scalloped shape is highlighted by a frill in the same fabric. The stripe also lines the white curtains.

▼ Have a break
Wallpapers with narrow stripes add height to a room, but if the effect is too dramatic, the horizontal elements of a dado or picture rail and wallpaper border will temper the effect.

furnishings. For floors in halls and on staircases, use striped runners in a flat herringbone or ribbed weave. These are traditional, hard-wearing and relatively inexpensive. They will protect the main flooring, and at the same time provide important decorative interest.

Country farmhouse
For a rustic, farmhouse look, choose plain stripes with simple wallpapers and natural materials. Plain, candy-striped wallpaper is ideal, and looks particularly attractive when used in conjunction with a dado rail. Use the stripe either above or below the dado rail, and team it with a plain version of the same colour.

Ticking, an old-fashioned utility cloth, with a characteristic herringbone weave, is an excellent fabric to use for this look. Originally hand-woven in linen as a covering for feather mattresses, it had to be sturdy and dense to keep the feathers in and, presumably, to keep the ticks out. Like many of the fabrics which have been with us a long time, ticking has been revamped in recent times to give it new qualities and is now available in many other colours besides the traditional black on white.

Coloured ticking looks just right made up as squab cushions on kitchen chairs. For a stunning, but unfussy bedroom treatment, a four-poster bed can be dressed in blue and white ticking – add a self-border with the stripes at right angles for a final flourish. A similarly dramatic effect can be achieved by using a plain fabric and lining it with ticking in the same colour plus white. This combination of plain and striped fabrics will work just as well for window treatments.

Striped tea cloth fabric, also known as glass cloth, is usually made of cotton, linen, or a mixture of both. It has a fresh, crisp texture which suits the simple country look, with colour-washed walls, and old pine or painted and distressed furniture. It is very effective for fresh bedroom curtains and valances, or you could use it in the kitchen for fresh curtains or tablecloths.

Muslin is another natural fabric which is just right for the informal country look. It comes self-striped or plain, natural or white. A self-striped ivory muslin, ideally with a silky finish, would make lovely billowing draperies on a four-poster bed and at the window.

Cottage stripes
For the country cottage look, co-ordinate stripes and florals, or choose combined stripe and floral designs. There are lots of co-ordinating ranges of fabrics and wallpapers available which include plain stripes, stripes with florals, small florals, mini-prints and plains. It is the combination of these which will achieve this look.

In cosy cottage rooms, where florals mixed with other florals would be too much, stripes provide pattern and texture without being overwhelming. You could combine a large floral print in strong or fresh colours with a sprig and stripe which includes two colours from the main fabric.

▲ Light relief
Striped cushions, trimmed with lace to soften their hard lines, help to break up the overall effect of the pattern on the bedspread. The window dressing combines both fabrics.

▼ Easy elegance
Ticking has an understated elegance and simplicity which is easy to live with. It's an inexpensive fabric, so use it in lavish quantities, with curtains spilling on to the floor.

Sophisticated stripes

The illusion of height given by stripes adds elegance to any room, and they are an ideal wall treatment for the more sophisticated country house look. On walls, however, avoid bumpy or uneven surfaces and rooms with odd angles as it will be difficult to get the stripes to line up, and irregularities will be only too obvious.

Stripes became very popular in the Regency period, around the end of the eighteenth century and the beginning of the nineteenth century. This style was essentially light and graceful, but suited to domestic interiors, unlike some of the rather grand styles which had preceded it. If you prefer antique or reproduction furniture and rather restrained surroundings, a Regency stripe or any fine multiple stripe will look wonderful in the reception areas of your home. Used in your living room it will create a light and airy atmosphere.

Keep the walls uncluttered – just one or two framed prints or paintings on each wall – and choose rather elaborate window treatments in plain or striped fabrics. The linear quality of elegant striped fabrics is particularly suited to elaborate draperies with lots of loops, gathers and swags, emphasizing the movement and flow of the fabric.

Textural stripes are ideal for upholstery because they add depth without fussiness. Used in these formal surroundings they look extremely smart.

▲ Elegant stripes
Striped wallpapers have an elegance which is perfect for the sophisticated country house look. Here, where stripes on the whole wall would make the room look too high, the effect is tempered with border papers and plainer paper.

▶ Rose-bud co-ordinates
A fine example of how to use a range of co-ordinated striped and floral fabrics: the main, rose-bud fabric is used for the curtains, and the motif is used again on the bedding with a striped background; the stripe alone makes a fine sheet and valance.

Country~style motifs

▲ In the farmyard
Farmyard animals and birds are some of the most popular country motifs. They can be found around the country-style home in a range of guises: on wallpapers, plates, tiles, and even as wooden cut-outs.

Animals and birds, fruits and vegetables, flowers and trees are just some of the images which fall into the category of country motifs. The images are everywhere in the country-style home: on textiles, wallpapers, tiles and china, and on purely decorative items like wooden cut-outs, ornaments, prints and paintings.

Sometimes a motif is used singly, but it may also make up part of a larger design, perhaps mixed with other country motifs or used with geometrics. Large designs may capture a whole country scene, such as the lovely Toile de Jouy fabrics from France, which are both charming and elegant.

Traditional patterns
Many of the most familiar country motifs have been used for hundreds of years to decorate the home, changing their form slightly to suit the fashion of each period of history. Classical motifs of horses, cats and mythological creatures were taken from the Ancient World. From Mediaeval paintings and tapestries came images of hunting scenes, animals and flowers, some of which, such as squirrels, thistles, strawberries and snails, are still familiar motifs in the contemporary country-style home.

Ideas were taken from China, India and the Middle East – all areas which had strong trading links with Europe. From China came peacocks, sprigs of peach and cherry blossom, waterlilies, tumbling mountain streams and scenes of everyday life. From India came designs of leaves and vines, and the 'tree of life' motif which is still widely used. From the Middle East came many of the

naturalistic designs we know, including scenes of flowers, birds and animals, gardens and trees.

At the end of the last century, the brilliant designers of the Arts and Crafts movement incorporated many motifs from Asia and the Middle East into their own flowing designs. The well-known peacock feather design, still produced by Liberty's, for example, is reminiscent of the peacock designs of China. Leafy images and the pine motif from India, which is now the basic motif in paisley

▲ *Cockerel tapestry cushion*

designs, were also widely adopted and modified by many designers.

These designs were taken from all sorts of things: rugs, fine hand-painted prints and wallpapers, decorative furniture and porcelain, which were all imported into Europe. Designers quickly adopted motifs taken from these imports, not just because they were attractive, but because they were popular and, by the late 19th century, some of these had been compiled in encyclopedias of ornamentation, providing inspiration for decorators and designers.

Popular interpretations

As designers continue to produce new products, decorative motifs are constantly being updated, so that most of the country motifs seen today are not replicas of the original designs, but modified versions adapted for the popular market.

The story of chintz makes a fine example of how motifs were copied, modified and developed. Chintz originally featured colourful Indian designs of plants and animals, but the fabric was such a huge success in Britain that local manufacturers started to produce imitations. They copied the overall feel of the designs and adopted some of the original motifs, such as exotic birds and hothouse flowers, but they also included their own motifs, based on British plants and flowers, birds, butterflies and small mammals.

Animals, birds and insects

Today's country-style homes contain motifs reflecting the countryside around them. Country manors abound with images of horses, dogs and hunting scenes, and of freshwater fish like trout and salmon – all images of favourite outdoor pursuits. Farmhouse or cottage style homes contain images of pigs, sheep and chickens, and of small country

creatures from the hedgerows, like field mice, hedgehogs, rabbits and squirrels.

Many of these animal motifs appear in new forms, but as a result of the increased interest in traditional styles, some of the old motifs are being copied or emulated. Wooden cut-outs of sheep, pigs and cows can be hung on the wall or propped up at the back of a shelf or kitchen worktop. These wooden cut-outs are often naively painted, sometimes following traditional designs and colours for a simple, rustic look.

Bird motifs, symbolizing life, peace and freedom, have been popular in many cultures and periods of the past. In Mediaeval times, the dove, with its biblical symbolism, was used in tapestries and even stained glass, as were common European birds like the wren. Later, the exotic birds depicted on Indian chintzes caught on, and today there is a wide range of motifs to choose from. Motifs of common birds, like robins or blue tits work well in a rustic, farmhouse style, as well as farmyard ducks, chickens and roosters, while more exotic birds like peacocks look best in the country house style.

The insects most commonly depicted

▲ *Spot the stencil*
A very rustic tablecloth, stencilled with a cockerel motif to match the spotted blue and white china, transforms an old pine table into a delightful place for tea. Large spots, also stencilled on to the cloth, emphasize the connection.

▼ *Flying ducks?*
A group of large china ducks makes a novel and rather special kitchen collection particularly as more can be added to the group as time goes by. Placed by an open window, they look as if they could take off into the sunshine.

in the country-style home are bees and butterflies. These colourful creatures recall sunny summer days, fresh breezes and the freedom of open spaces. For the kitchen, look out for bee and honey pot motifs on tea towels and china – these motifs will also go down well in a child's room. Choose pale wallpapers with butterfly motifs for a fresh, airy feel in bedrooms and bathrooms. For an elegant effect, choose two or three colour fabrics with bee or butterfly motifs, and combine them with fabrics depicting flowers or even vines.

Flowers, fruits and vegetables

Flowers have an enduring appeal which has made them popular motifs since early times. In the Mediaeval period, a type of tapestry called *mille fleur* was developed, which got its name from the millions of flowers that filled in the background. The famous Lady and the Unicorn tapestries from France belong

▲ Hopping mad
Co-ordinated bunny fabrics on the valance, cushion cover and bedhead are combined with a matching wallpaper to make this an endearing country bedroom for a young girl.

▼ Butterfly elegance
An elegant fabric in ivory and plum with motifs of butterflies, leaves and flowers complements the dark wood of this formal dining table and gives the room a fresh country feel.

to this group. Kits for making copies of these tapestries for wall hangings and cushion covers are available today and, because of their detailed backgrounds, they are fun to make as well as a pleasure to look at.

Spring flowers make excellent subjects for fresh fabrics like chintz, for painted fire screens and tiles. Use a flowery chintz with a pale background for bedroom curtains to create a delicate freshness, and place a tapestry cushion featuring similar flowers on a bedroom chair to continue the theme. If there is a fireplace, white tiles with spring flower motifs or a painted flower screen will complete the look.

Autumnal fruits like apples, peaches and plums, with their rich colours ranging from greeny-yellow and pale orange to deep purple, make wonderful, mouthwatering country motifs, which

are particularly appropriate in kitchens and dining rooms. Use fruity fabrics in these rooms for curtains and chair covers, or for a colourful tablecloth. Look out for tea towels with fruit motifs and kitchen accessories like oven gloves, tea cosies or even an apron.

For the dining room, look for wallpaper borders which pick up the fruity theme, or make a stencil by tracing motifs from fabric, and use this to make your own borders. Coloured drawings or botanical prints of fruits are another option, and will look particularly good in a formal dining room. For the table, you could have pretty china or earthenware with fruit motifs, like the Portmeirion ranges.

Vegetable motifs are often used in the kitchen on wallpapers and tea towels, but tapestries with vegetable motifs will make eccentric cushion covers for a sofa or armchair, and can be combined with fruit, flower, bird or animal tapestry cushions for a country feel. Bowls and plates, which have vegetable motifs or which are textured to look like vegetables, can be used to hold pot plants, store pot pourri or simply as decoration.

◄ Dining room delight
A luscious fruit fabric with a fresh, white background transforms the window into a blaze of colour, and calls attention to the fruit china on the window-sill. The same fabric in another colour-way is used for a co-ordinated tablecloth.

▲ Kitchen kit
A glorious red, yellow and green tapestry panel of apples and apple blossom makes a striking wall decoration. The panel is made from a tapestry kit.

▼ Mouthwatering
A collection of fruity china makes a mouthwatering display in the kitchen, highlighted by the dark wood shelves. The china will also look nice when it's in use in the dining room.

▲ Fruits, flowers and vines
A striking grape vine fabric, used for the curtains and chair cover, provides the most obvious country motifs here, but close inspection reveals that the carpet covered with its fern and ivy designs also has its own country style. The small box under the table adds emphasis to the fruity theme, and fresh fruits and flowers complete the look.

◄ Daisy ways
Traditional large country motifs are still popular in the country-style home: this fabric, of the Michaelmas daisy, is an original William Morris design. Notice the clever trimming idea on the cushion where the decorative buttons have each been covered with a daisy motif.

▼ Tile style
The large pattern on the blue and green tiles creates a striking effect and provide a colour link with the vegetable china on the wall. Used as a border, the tiles add life to this farmhouse kitchen.

Toile de Jouy

These pictorial designs were developed in 1770 at the Jouy factory near Versailles, in France, and depict scenes like merry milkmaids, shepherds watching their sheep, or lovers strolling arm in arm through the countryside.

The fabrics are printed in a single colour on a white, off-white or creamy background, and the colours are soft and mellow, based on the original natural dyes. Pinks and pinky-reds, blues and rusts, earth green, brown and black are the traditional colours. The misty colours of the fabric and the pale backgrounds combine to create an elegant effect which can look lovely in formal bedrooms or dining rooms.

Toile de Jouy fabrics are large prints, and like other large prints should be used carefully. Use them for curtains, flat blinds and bedspreads where the whole pattern can be seen.

◄ Toile de Jouy
A traditional Toile de Jouy fabric, showing romantic figures ambling through the countryside, looks delightful used on extensive soft furnishings. The large pattern on these traditional fabrics can make them difficult to use. They tend to look best in a spacious room where you can stand back to admire the design.

▼ Traditional blue motif

INDEX

Page numbers in *italic* refer to picture captions

Acknowledgements

Photographers: 7 IPC Magazines/Robert Harding Picture Library, 8(bl,cr) Eaglemoss Publications/Graham Rae, 8(br), 8-9(t) 9(br) IPC Magazines/Robert Harding Picture Library, 9(bl), 10(t) Eaglemoss Publications/Graham Rae, 10(bl) The Merchant Tiler, 10(r) Sanderson, 11(br) IPC Magazines/Robert Harding Picture Library, 11(cr) Eaglemoss Publications/Graham Rae, 12(t) Sanderson, 12(b) Elizabeth Whiting Associates/Nick Carter, 13 Eaglemoss Publications/Steve Tanner, 15(b) Welbeck PR/Dulux, 16(l) Eaglemoss Publications/Steve Tanner, 16-17 Liberty, 18(t) Ken Kirkwood, 18(bl) Ronseal, 18(br), 19 Eaglemoss Publications/Steve Tanner, 20(t) Crown/Charles Barber Lyons, 20(b) Ken Kirkwood, 20-21 Sanderson, 22, 23(t) Welbeck PR/Dulux, 23(br) Crown/Charles Barber Lyons, 24(tl) Elizabeth Whiting Associates/Di Lewis, 24(br) Sanderson, 25 Tif Hunter, 26(t) Crown/Charles Barber Lyons, 26(bl) Swish/Welbeck PR, 26(br) Elizabeth Whiting Associates/Rodney Hyett, 27(t) Robert Harding Picture Library, 27(b) Arcaid/Julie Phipps, 28(t) Elizabeth Whiting Associates/Di Lewis, 28(b), 29(t) Crown/Charles Barber Lyons, 29(b) Elizabeth Whiting Associates/Spike Powell, 30(t) Modes et Travaux, 30(b) Crown/Charles Barber Lyons, 31 Tif Hunter, 32(bl) Richard Paul, 32-33 Elizabeth Whiting Associates, 33(tr) Bo Appeltofft, 33(br) Elizabeth Whiting Associates/Spike Powell, 34(t) Ken Kirkwood, 34(br) Mal Stone, 35 Tif Hunter, 36, 37, 38(tl) Richard Paul, 38(tr) Elizabeth Whiting Associates/Neil Lorimer, 38(b) Elizabeth Whiting Associates/June Buck, 39(t) Mondadoripress/Buratti-Xerra, 39(bl) Whiteheads Fabrics, 39(br) Cristal Tiles, 40(t,br) Rene Stoeltie, 40(bl) Elizabeth Bradley Designs, 41 Ideal Standard, 42(t) 100 Idees/Bianchi-Schoumacher, 42(b) Houses & Interiors, 43(tr) Dulux/Welbeck PR, 43(bl) Deidi von Schaewan, 43(br) Kingfisher/Chilmark PR, 44(t) Houses & Interiors, 44(b) Ken Kirkwood, 45(t) Maison Marie Claire/Nicolas-Postic, 45(b) Crown/Charles Barber Lyons, 46(t) Crowson Fabrics, 46(bl) Elizabeth Whiting Associates/Michael Dunne, 46(br) Ametex/Welbeck PR, 47(bl) Marks & Spencer, 47(cr) Eaglemoss Publications/Steve Tanner, 48(t) Marks & Spencer, 48(b) Eaglemoss Publications/Steve Tanner, 49(tr,b) Dorma, 50 Paper Moon, 51-56 Sanderson, 57 Eaglemoss Publications/Steve Tanner, 58, 59(t) Sanderson, 59(b) Elizabeth Whiting Associates/Spike Powell, 60(t) Tomkinson's Carpets, 60(b) Dorma, 61 Eaglemoss Publications/Simon Page-Ritchie, 62 Stoddard/Candor PR, 63(tl) Eaglemoss Publications/Steve Tanner, 63(tr,br) Laura Ashley Home, 63(bl) Ken Kirkwood, 64 Sanderson, 65(tr) Elizabeth Whiting Associates/Spike Powell, 65(cl) Laura Ashley Home, 65(b) Richard Paul, 66(tl) Ashton & Dean (MFI)/Spa PR, 66(br) Elizabeth Whiting Associates/Tom Leighton, 67 Eaglemoss Publications/Simon Page-Ritchie, 68 Sanderson, 69(tl) Richard Paul, 69(b) Warner Fabrics, 70(t) Richard Paul, 70(b) Elizabeth Whiting Associates/Neil Lorimer, 71 Eaglemoss Publications/Simon Page-Ritchie, 72(tr) Elizabeth Whiting Associates/Di Lewis, 72(b) Rene Stoeltie, 73(r) Hill & Knowles, 73(bl) Eaglemoss Publications/Simon Page-Ritchie, 74(t) Sterling Roncraft, 74(br) Eaglemoss Publications/Simon Page-Ritchie, 75(tl) Elizabeth Whiting Associates/Spike Powell, 75(tr) Ken Kirkwood, 75(bl) Eaglemoss Publications/Simon Page-Ritchie, 75(br) Elizabeth Whiting Associates/ Michael Dunne, 76(tl) Anna French, 76(tr) Habitat, 76(b) The Nursery Window, 77 Eaglemoss Publications/Steve Tanner, 78(t) Robert Harding Picture Library, 78(b) Richard Paul, 79(t) Elizabeth Whiting Associates/Di Lewis, 79(b) Elizabeth Whiting Associates/Brian Harrison, 80(t) Mondadoripress/Zanelli-Costa, 80(b) Elizabeth Whiting Associates/Jerry Tubby, 81(cl) Laura Ashley Home, 81(cr,b) Elizabeth Whiting Associates/Michael Crockett, 82(t) Elizabeth Whiting Associates/ Andreas von Einsiedel, 82(c) Dorma, 82(b) Richard Paul, 83 Eaglemoss Publications/ John Suett, 84(tl) Bo Appeltofft, 84(bl) Laura Ashley Home, 84-85 Crown/Charles Barber Lyons, 86(tl) Jahreszeiten-Verlag/Peter Adams, 86(b) Harriet's House, 87(t) Elizabeth Whiting Associates/Tom Leighton, 87(bl) Maison Marie Claire/Girandeau-Postic, 87(br) Eaglemoss Publications/Steve Tanner, 88(t) Dovedale Fabrics, 88(bl) Eaglemoss Publications/Steve Tanner, 88(br) Dorma, 89, 90(tl) Eaglemoss Publications/John Suett, 90(tr) Ariadne Holland, 90(b) Sue Atkinson/Arc Studios, 91(t) Elizabeth Whiting Associates/Michael Crockett, 91(c) Eaglemoss Publications/John Suett, 91(b) Laura Ashley Home, 92(tl) Eaglemoss Publications/John Suett, 92(bl) Textra, 92-93(c) Anna French, 93(t) Ehrman, 93(b) Marks & Spencer, 94(t) Sanderson, 94(c) Sue Atkinson/Arc Studios, 94(bl) Ametex, 94(br) Eaglemoss Publications/John Suett.